After the Ball is Over
Mardi Gras Designer Larry Youngblood looks back on his 50 Years of Costumes and Memories

Completed and edited posthumously by Elizabeth Y. Canik

Published by
Elizabeth Canik
Covington, Louisiana 70435

Copyright © 2012 by Elizabeth Y. Canik
All rights reserved. No part of this publication may be reproduced or transmitted in any form or by any means, electronic or mechanical, including photocopy, recording, or any information storage and retrieval system, without permission in writing from the copyright owner.

ISBN 978-1-61863-430-6

Printed in the United States of America

Dedication

I dedicate this book to the memory of my parents, Irene and Captain Peter R. Youngblood, Sr., for supporting me in a career choice no "Bywater" boy ever pursued, and to my big brother, Peter, who always had my back no matter what.

Acknowledgments
(From Larry's niece Elizabeth)

Many thanks go to those who assisted me with the completion of this book. To Jessica Lewis who, with her amazing camera, beautifully photographed all design sketches and photographs; to Jennifer Green for patiently transferring the manuscript into her publishing program and more; to Wayne Phillips who provided additional historical information about Mardi Gras krewes and remained patient with me during my lengthy "Q & A" sessions; to my good friend, Missy French, for assisting me with research, and to Dianne Canik for her editing assistance and being my second set of eyes.

I treasure the memories of my uncle, Larry Youngblood, and my parents, Peter and Sera Youngblood, whose love of Mardi Gras inspired me to finish what Larry started. Most importantly I cherish my husband Jimmy, and children, Adam and Sera, who always inspire and support me.

Foreword

It was always Larry Youngblood's wish to one day publish a story about his life as a Mardi Gras designer complete with all of the backstage drama that unfolded while dealing with the characters with whom he was so involved throughout his career. He wrote, edited, destroyed and started over several times but his personal life, being the proverbial train wreck, did not allow him to complete his manuscript. Over time, his dream became notes and pictures shoved in a box to be replaced by other events he put to paper, particularly his life in the United States Air Force during the Korean War. In those memoirs he told of how his brother, Peter, rescued him from the fate that should have resulted from his mischievous antics. Thanks to Larry's third wife, Ruth, those writings literally went up in flames. Their life together could be a book in and of itself, but let's not go there.

In 1998 Larry suffered a massive stroke that ended his career as a designer. While he retained his creative ability, sadly, the designs in his mind would never come to life on paper or otherwise. I am Larry's niece, Liz, and whenever I visited him I brought a variety of his sketches to cheer him up. His memory of each drawing was amazing. He was able to relate to me every detail of each sketch, the associated carnival club, and often, the names of the maid or duke who wore the costume. He recalled both hilarious situations along with events he would prefer to forget altogether.

Our meetings and conversations resulted in renewed interest in his incomplete manuscript. This book has been compiled to impart his insights as a designer and the highlights of events and mishaps throughout his fifty year career, many of which were recorded exactly as he told them to me. Other stories have been pieced together from his notes following his death. Also included are sketches of some of his most beautiful creations.

Distasteful events also played out behind the dressing room doors of captains, the kings and queens and in the krewe quarters. Such topics are listed as chapters, though while certainly enticing, will not be found in this book:

- *The King Is Doing What? Does He Know She is Only 16?*
- *I Think an Ice Pack Under the Queen's Crown Will Show*
- *Honey, We Can't Hold Up the Ball Because Maid #6 Can't Stop Throwing Up!*
- *What Do You Mean You Can't Wake Up the King?*
- *The Queen Went Where? When Will She Be Back?*

- *The Queen Won't Come Down Until the King Apologizes for What?*
- *What Do You Mean the Captain's Gown Isn't Finished Yet? It's 8:45!*
- *I Don't Care If He Is the King's Grandson- -He Can't Go Out Like That. He Peed In His Tights!*

Larry spoke fondly of most carnival club captains with whom he worked through the years. Many were his dearest friends. Of course, there were those who were always difficult and very hard to please. As a result, some clubs for whom Larry designed will not be mentioned by name, the captains and club owners preferring the details of their club activities not be specifically presented. Average Mardi Gras fans are unaware of the behind-the-scenes antics and events leading up to the big night of a carnival ball, so in Larry's words, worth repeating, and through his memories and costumes, worth sharing, I hope to convey his experiences as a designer.

The costumes illustrated in this book do not necessarily coincide with the story being recounted.

The remainder of this "Foreword" is in Larry's words exactly as he dictated them to me hoping that his story as a designer would one day be told:

I can think of nothing I would rather have done than design fashion and costumes in New Orleans. It was the most exciting and challenging career choice with never any breaks. The 50's, 60's and 70's were my best designing years. There were more balls than there are now, and there was a great auditorium to hold such events. But I look back and loved every minute of it. It has been one long, beautiful and fun ride.

Many thanks go to all those who through the years helped and supported me in my career and private life, the club owners, captains, dressmakers and behind-the-scenes people; my dearest friends, Pip and Barbara Brennan, Steve and Barbara Johnson, all their wonderful families and so many others; Roger, Buddy, Ed and all the guys from the National Guard unit, and most of all my family, my late parents, Peter and Irene, for sharing my vision and keeping me in art supplies and lessons at a time when there was little money; my three big brothers, Peter, Tom and Bobby, who always thought my parents brought the wrong baby home from the hospital when I was born but who ultimately supported me; my nephew, Patrick, who shares my love of Mardi Gras and my niece, Elizabeth, who is helping to piece all of this together. God bless you all.

In The Beginning

The costume sketches Lawrence (Larry) Youngblood drew as a child in 1937 made him laugh years later as a popular Mardi Gras costume designer in New Orleans. At the time, though, he thought he was great. Having no known artistic ability in either family tree, my grandparents wondered about the origin of his talent.

Larry about age 10, 1938 as king of a children's Mardi Gras ball.

The first musical and ice shows Larry attended had him hooked. His heart belonged to Sonja Henie, Ruby Keeler, Joan Blondell, Maria Montez, Lupe Velez, Dolores Del Rio, Ginger Rogers, and yes, Anna Mae Wong. In the 30's, even in black and white, the costumes were spectacular, but with the advent of Technicolor, after enjoying a movie, he would leave the theater, go home and draw his heart out. At that time, he was still attending art school at the Delgado Museum of Art where his teacher took a dim view of a tranquil lagoon scene with trees and bridges suddenly being invaded by chorus girls dressed from the movie *42nd Street*. Larry was kindly told that what went on in the movies did not apply to the hallowed halls of the Delgado Museum. In class he, indeed, drew the nude figures of classic statues, and later, from live nude models, but he drew them with feathers in their rears and musical notes on their bare bellies.

Larry also loved the lavish period costume of such epics as *Robin Hood, Elizabeth* and *Essex, Marie Antoinette* and *Gone with the Wind*. He watched them over and over just for the costumes. And what were all his friends watching? Rin Tin Tin, Buck Jones, Hoot Gibson, Gene Autry and Roy Rogers. Larry would ask, "Why watch a bunch of dumb cowboys chase a bunch of dumb Indians when I could watch dozens of half naked girls singing, dancing and playing harps, huge glass pianos and Ruby Keeler, Dick Powell, Joan Blondell and Jack Oakie popping out of a two story fountain without getting a drop of water on them?"

He felt he was ready for Hollywood at twelve years old. Not only would he have designed the costumes and scenery, but if my grandmother had her way, he would have starred in the production, too. Early on she and my grandfather, realizing his talent, supported Larry's passion for drawing. All too often she was called to his elementary school to meet with the principal, because Larry had drawn naked women on the biceps of his male classmates. My grandmother never lost her cool. She simply looked at the art work on the boys' arms, noted that the drawings were even better than the ones he had done the previous week and told him to keep up the good work. Needless to say, the nuns were not amused.

During World War II Larry sent his versions of pin-up girls to his three older brothers, Peter, Tom and Bobby, who were overseas at the same time but in different parts of the world. They all dutifully wrote back that he was as good as George Petty, the artist famous for the "Petty Girl." Of course, Larry felt they were right. He never did get the hang of humble.

The 4 Youngblood boys, L to R- Tom, Larry, Bobby and Peter in 1955.

In addition to art studies, he had taken singing and dancing lessons since the age of four. He also took accordion lessons for six years, and eventually played for the USO. He loved it all and was good at everything he tried. He expressed fond memories of my grandmother making costumes for him and his dancing partners for reviews in the late 1930's:

> *I was always very interested in the sewing of costumes my mother would make for me and some little girl dancing partner for a revue. Very bright, each sequin caught with a bugle bead and rhinestone fringe done by hand so it would glitter and catch the light when we moved. I had a few ideas myself so my*

mom would try it and if it didn't look good she could rip it out. My father would doze in his big chair with Jack, our big dog at his feet always alert for when a bugle bead would hit the floor. My mother had a goose-neck lamp on the dining room table and a large piece of black felt spread out. My job was to assort the sequins by color and size, keep the beading needles threaded and punch rhinestones on the satin or velvet. I was always amazed that my mother would put a whole pile of the beads in her mouth, pop one bead out at a time, catch it with the needle and put it to the costume. She would repeat this process over and over and not once did she ever swallow a bead or stitch her lip.

Larry started designing ladies gowns while still in high school at Francis T. Nicholls. He designed dresses for dances, balls and weddings for his friends, girlfriends and for debutantes. Horace Russ, Larry's art teacher from school and later privately, taught him how to dye fabric using the *Batik* method. Larry dyed pieces of fabric then designed a dress specifically for the fabric. The result was amazing and rich with color, something from which he never shied away. He loved designing gowns and costumes using vibrant colors and was not afraid to use unusual combinations.

Costumes by Larry Youngblood (right) are fitted on Miss Emogene Gunter by Mrs. Emily Crawford, seamstress

Larry preparing a production for New Orleans Recreation Department (NORD) in the 1950's.

He also studied fashion design in New York at the Franklin School of Art which led to a successful career in New Orleans at D.H. Holmes and Kreeger's department stores. He wrote a fashion column for the *Times Picayune* newspaper and was a featured player on *Dawn Busters*, a local radio program. He did quite well for being so young, not yet twenty two.

Always patriotic and wanting to do his part, he joined the Air Force before the Korean War. Although stationed state-side, he found time to put together Air Force musical stage productions using male and female military personnel as entertainers. He wrote, directed, starred in and designed all of the events, his efforts producing hits well received by audiences. Returning home, he attended the John McCrady Art School in the French Quarter on the GI Bill while continuing to design for carnival clubs and private clients.

Larry started officially designing Mardi Gras costumes at eighteen years old, the Krewe of Carrollton being his first big club. About forty krewes later, he was still going strong. While designing costumes he also designed weddings, 'Spring Fiesta' gowns, high fashion for steady clients and served as the New Orleans Recreation Department's Costume Director for twenty years. His career kept him very busy--designing weddings alone could have been one entire career. He once

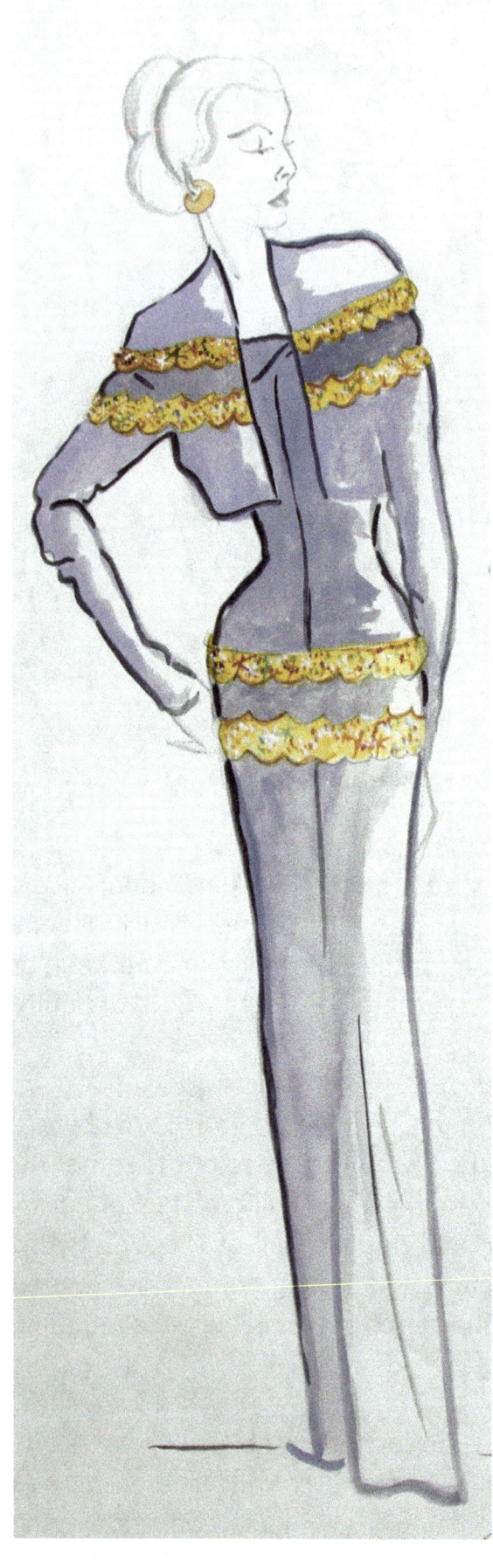

told me he designed a huge wedding for a prominent Italian family in New Orleans. There were thirteen bridesmaids each wearing a different colored dress. He joked that he ran out of colors and had to make some up. The wedding was so large the bride was on her honeymoon before the last bridesmaid exited the church.

I asked him which krewes were his favorites as far as his best design work was concerned. He named Carrollton, Iris, Elenians and Bacchus, but he felt his most spectacular work as an artist was represented in the Krewe of Virgilians. Because Larry was such a stickler for authenticity, a tremendous amount of time was spent researching topics and themes before he drew one line on a sketch. Long before computers made research so simple, he was a "regular" at the public and university libraries.

Mardi Gras is a year round industry, not just a seasonal one. Often Larry was finishing one set of sketches while beginning new designs for the same krewe for the following year. Often krewe captains knew what their themes would be two years in advance.

In the 1960's, while staying at my grandmother's, I often watched Larry and sometimes helped him prepare for sketching sessions. He had a particular routine he always followed. On the large dining room table he placed all of his supplies, paper, paint pots, pencils, reference books and notes. He made a pitcher of vodka martinis and, finally, he put a few popular records on the hi-fi. Two hours later the pitcher was empty, he had produced twenty or so beautiful, complete sketches and he didn't miss a beat. It was an amazing thing to watch.

High fashion from the late 1940's and early 1950's

Broadway Memory

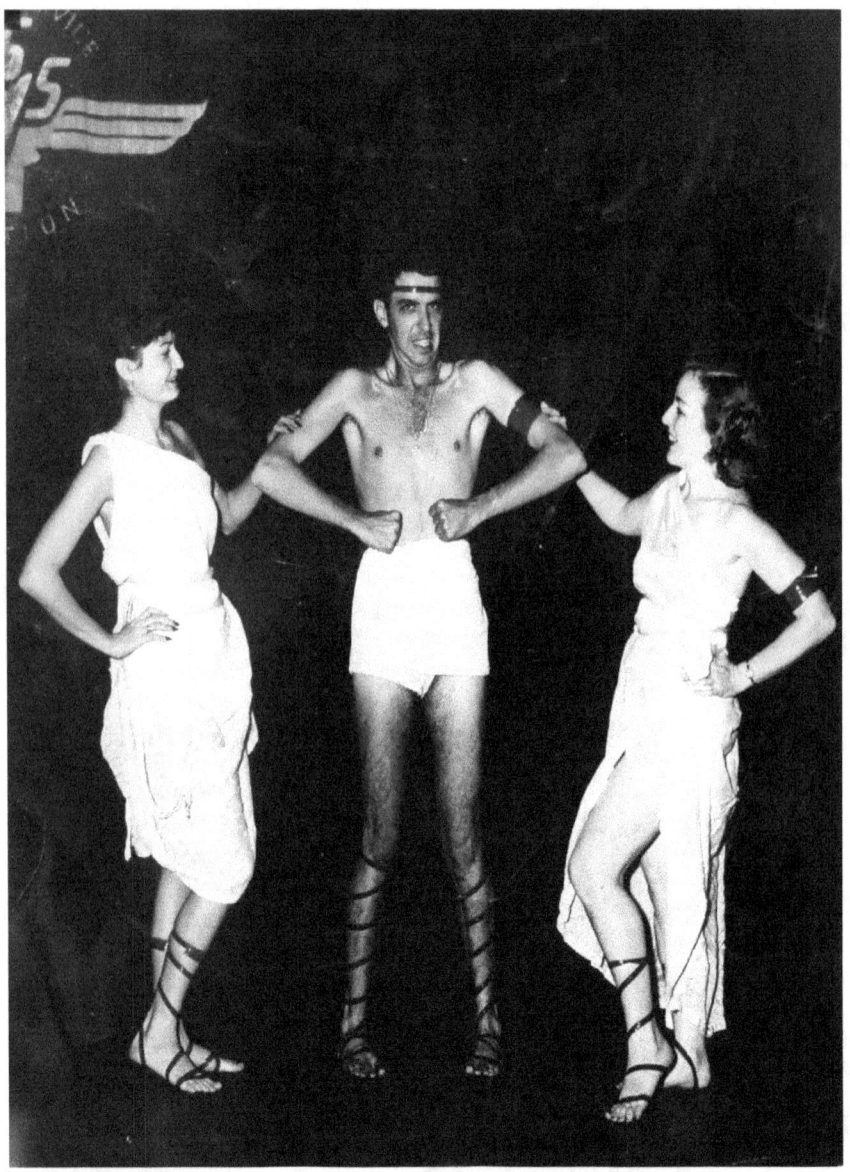

Larry in his comedic role as Icarus, surrounded by Grecian beauties (WAFS) in the Air Force musical he wrote, designed and starred in 1951 in Langley, VA. Since the budget for the musicals was small, they had to be very creative with costumes and scenery. Here, sandals are made of electrical tape and the togas of silk parachutes.

To Larry, Mardi Gras balls were a form of show business. His cast was the carnival krewe, his director was the captain, and the court, king and queen were his stars. From the box seats to the third balcony, the audience was just like that of a Broadway show, only in New York a ticket could cost a small fortune and in New Orleans all you needed was an invitation. Invitations for some of the balls, however, were as hard to come by as any big show on Broadway. On this subject, he recalled:

I remember in the early 50's, I was in New York on leave from the Air Force and a dear friend, Lou Stoneman, who handled many of my fabrics, also supplied fabrics for the biggest Broadway shows, ice shows and Radio City Music Hall performers. He was the most wonderful man and his shop, a warehouse in the Garment District right off of 7th Avenue, was quite a sight to see for a new designer like me. If he didn't have it, he could get it, and if he couldn't get, it hadn't been invented yet. One day while I was there looking at fabrics, the likes of which I had never seen in my life, he got a phone call and said, "Yeah, I can be there in about half an hour. Oh, I got a friend I wanna bring, Jerry Youngmen. He is in the Air Force, but he is also a fabulous costume designer for the Mardi Gras in New OR-LEANS!" (For some reason Lou always called me Jerry instead of Larry and Youngmen instead of Youngblood.) He would laugh and say, "A Gentile ya might be, but a Jew you look like 'Blue Eyes', believe me!"

We jumped into a cab and arrived at a very dreary, run-down building where a freight elevator took us to the workshop of Madam Keniskir, a Russian-Jewish seamstress, who was making the costumes for Auntie Mame designed by the legendary Irene Schraff, who was the top costume designer on the "Great White Way." The thought of meeting this legend was exciting enough, but who should be there for two fittings for the show but its star, Rosalind Russell, who was not only gracious and beautiful but also very interested in hearing all about Mardi Gras. She had never been to it but was dying to see it all. Irene Schraff actually envied me designing for something as exciting as Mardi Gras, something new and different all the time. But I stammered, "Broadway, beautiful stars like Miss Russell, why that's what all costume designers dream of!" "Honey", she said as she removed several pins from her mouth, "I love it, but if this show is a hit, why Roz here will wear this same costume for two or three years." "I'll drink to that", Miss Russell said laughing. Irene then said, "What I mean is, we'll make her new versions of the same costume, that's how it is with long running shows on Broadway. Now, of course, if they decide to do a movie of it and pick me up as the designer, well darling, that's a whole new ball game. I'll still do the same design but on a much more elaborate scale, because it will be seen by millions. And besides that, I might get a shot for an Oscar for best costume designer." It was hard to believe. Here I was having a conversation with one of Broadway's most sought after costume designers and one of Hollywood's finest leading ladies. Not bad for a designer, who had not yet reached his twenty-first birthday to even be in this fabulous company.

Larry (front with a girlfriend on lap) surrounded by fellow airmen and WAFS about 1951 in Langley, VA.

But as great as all that was, the fact remained that Larry Youngblood was an Airman First Class in the United States Air Force on active duty stationed at Langley Air Force Base, Virginia, and Mardi Gras, Broadway and everything else would have to wait until the Korean War was over.

Larry and fellow airman preparing for Air Force musical, about 1951 in Langley, VA.

I Want to Start a Club

Through the years many men and women asked Larry's advice about how to start a carnival club and asked him to design the costumes. He always tried to get them to talk to well established captains of other krewes, but the truth was no captain, male or female, was interested in the competition. As it was, he often acted as a referee between krewe captains whose parades were on the same day but in different parts of the city, purposely done to draw crowds away from the other krewe. Unfortunately, Larry was designer for both and could not be in two places at once. He told them that if they could not work out their silly differences he would not design for either one of them. So, one club would reluctantly reschedule their parade at a different time on the same day allowing crowds to attend both parades.

Larry would walk future club owners through the process of creating a club. He would explain how expensive and time consuming organizing a club could be, along with set-backs, disappointments and the possibility of the occasional bout with ulcers, high blood pressure and heart problems. Larry met some of the strangest people as a result, and he told me:

> *I met some of the strangest fruit cakes of all time. Frankly speaking, the crazy ones are not all locked up. This one sunny, Sunday afternoon in the early 60's, I was to meet, let's just call her Mrs. Cynthia Flukewoode who had great dreams of a ball and parade with both men and women in the krewe and she and her husband, Chester, as co-captains. A co-ed krewe was unheard of by anyone, except the Krewe of Elks, a family group who followed Rex on Mardi Gras day on wonderfully decorated trucks. Granted it was one way to keep a family together, but an afternoon parade after Rex and before Comus, was a little far out, even for me. Let me describe Mrs. Flukewoode. Well, she was a cross between Kate Smith and Sophie Tucker, only bigger and shorter with the most brilliant red hair I had ever seen, and as ladies were still wearing hats then, a dark green mass of feathers caught up in her buns, rats and plaits. The hat dipped to one side complete with veil which she never bothered to lift, and it hit her right at her nose. She was wearing her best Joan Crawford suit with the huge shoulder pads in an interesting shade of green, lots of jewelry all being supported by her tiny, tiny feet. Chester on the other hand looked like a very*

skinny, funeral director all in black, not much hair left and had the saddest blue eyes I have ever seen. He looked like he was ready to cry! After I explained all the tragic pitfalls of forming a carnival krewe, I smiled and sat back. "NONSENSE, dear boy!" she roared. "We are going to revolutionize the whole carnival scene. We will feature the young and the physically perfect to everyone. Our plans are to do the first Olympics in glorious Rome. What do you think of that?" "Well, that is different all right," I responded. "But they didn't wear many clothes back then so designing costumes could be a challenge." She said, "No, no dear boy, we will have exquisitely healthy, young people, perfect in every way. We don't want to cover their bodies with velvets and satins. Your job should be easy, we don't want much on them at all, do we Chester?" "No my dear," he meekly replied. I took a long sip of my martini, and naturally thought to myself, these two pecans have escaped from Jackson and are now sitting in my living room. "Well, Mrs. Flukewoode, this is a fantastic idea. But you will have to get someone to design your floats and the scenery in the auditorium. This could cost a lot of money." "Not to worry my dear boy, let's start with a sketch of the king and queen first, then we can figure out who the gods and goddesses will be and what exciting sports events we'll depict and, of course, the costumes for Chester and me. They should be very, very different," she barked. My mind was racing wildly at the thought of this woman in a one-shoulder chiffon to the knee, and Chester in an Olympic jock strap with rhinestones, all one hundred and twenty pounds of him! "What, what will you all represent?" I asked weakly, while my stomach churned and I felt the beginning of a nasty headache. "Why, Mr. Youngblood, I see myself as 'Minerva' the Goddess of Wisdom, Art and Warfare, and Chester? Why, Chester will be the greatest of the gods, ZEUS! What do you think of that?" she said as she stood up triumphantly. That's all brother, was what I thought. "Well now, what can I say? I mean, that's really something; I don't think I've ever heard of anything quite like it," I replied as I got a little lightheaded. "Well then, you'll do it. Chester, give Mr. Youngblood two hundred and fifty dollars on account. Well now wait, oh! I realize it's going to cost much more than that! Oh, I do, but this is just to show our good faith," she said. As they both got up, Chester put two crisp one hundred dollar bills in my hand and five tens. "But wait, Mrs. Flukewoode, Mr. Flukewoode, wait," I protested. As they got to my front door - - "We'll call you, dear boy, remember the body is a beautiful thing.

Show it in all its exquisite form. Bye!" she said as she waved, and they were gone. If I didn't have the money in my hand I would have believed maybe this whole scene had never happened, but there were three glasses on the table, my notebook with notes and a slight scent of Mrs. Flukewoode's heavy perfume in the air. Dear God, what have I let myself in for? A ball and parade of health nuts, a nudist colony coming out in the open maybe? Well, I'd like to think I'm an honorable man, so I drew a king and queen, and yes, even Mrs. Flukewoode as 'Minerva.' I never did do Chester. As thin as he was, I just didn't know how to even approach it. But then the strangest thing happened. They didn't come back, call or even send a letter. I put the money in the bank and looked in the phone book and asked around. No one, but no one, had ever heard of them. Were they from out of town or out of this world? To this day, I have never seen or heard from the Flukewoodes again."

Larry in his studio in the early 1960's.

The Queen Who Would Be Queen Again and Again and Again

Larry described to me the next character as one with whom he dealt, unfortunately, about a dozen times. Many readers may recognize her, but her real name is not used:

Camilla LeDuke loved being queen of a ball, queen of a parade, queen of anything. As long as she was queen she didn't care and money was no object. When I first met her in the late 40's I was impressed. She was owner of a very famous French Quarter restaurant. It was said her late father was the last of French royalty and settled in New Orleans. CRAP, CRAP and more CRAP! He was no more a duke than my dog was and Camilla was no more the daughter of a French duke than my great aunt Rose.

When hard times hit, her father was persuaded to open an elegant little French restaurant where all the right people gathered. Of course, the restaurant was and still is a fine one. When I first met Camilla in 1949, she was queen of a small but beautiful ladies organization (no parade) composed mostly of middle-aged and older ladies. The theme was an Austrian one which took place in the Victorian period with pretty gowns, sweeping trains, "Gibson Girl" hair-dos and a garden party, all very lovely. Dear Camilla was supposed to be a visiting queen from Sweden, very pastel, pink or rose lace and silk all worked in sequins and beads. That's how I designed it anyway.

I was still a new designer and had never worked with the dressmaker, an elderly French lady whose word was law. I was simply told it was all very pretty, patted on the head and told to get lost, which I did. In those days I did what I was told.

Things seemed to go smoothly. The ball started and there was the garden of a castle, flowers and trees, little white grill work chairs and benches, the krewe in period gowns and soldiers and waiters serving wine to the guests, all played by women, of course. The maids came out, some with fans, others with umbrellas, all very pretty. Then the queen came, dear Camilla. It would seem that she and the dressmaker felt my design was too pale for words, so they decided to jazz it up. She was still in pink lace alright, but also gigantic fuchsia roses the size of dinner plates, and lavender bows, flounces of pink, rose and fuchsia tulle coming out of some of the strangest places, all sequined. She had a lace collar with pink and

Queen, Krewe of Alpheus late 1940's

fuchsia plumes and a crown so high I was surprised it didn't get caught in the drapes hanging from the second floor balcony! It was a monument to bad taste and so overdone it was sickening. However, dear Camilla, shaking her black dyed curls and over-made face, thought she was fantastic. The audience didn't seem to mind, as I was to find out later, that many of them would be invited to the queen's dressing room later for free champagne and goodies. This was my first time with Camilla as queen, and I hoped it would be my last. As my bad luck would have it, I would have dear Camilla as my queen no less than ten times between 1949 and 1975. We did not hit it off at all. I found her overbearing, she had a vile temper, was a heavy drinker, abusive and had a vocabulary that would make a sailor blush--and those were her good points! I was so proud to see "Costumes designed by Larry Youngblood" in the ball programs until I saw what dear Camilla did to her gowns so many times.

One year, in a men's club, Camilla's costume represented champagne and the king red wine. The costumes were stunning, and by this time I had enough experience that I saw to it Camilla could not bribe the dressmaker. The captain was on my side, too, which helped. She looked very pretty with the jeweled grapes cascading down her gown. The whole trellis effect done in rhinestones was stunning. She was reasonably sober, mean, but sober. The big problem, though, was that the king couldn't stand her guts and showed it! Sometimes you get a king and queen who really show their dislike for each other, especially in the grand march where the king and queen acknowledge the audience on both lower and upper floors. For instance, the king will step forward and acknowledge the box seat sections, catching the queen off guard, and so she also waves her scepter downward while he switches his greeting to the audience upstairs, putting his scepter right in front of her face, which pisses her off to no end, then they reverse the waves. Another little trick a king does to an unloved queen is to look down from the corner of his eye and plant his foot right on the side of her gown so that when she tries to move forward, she can't. She sways back and forth, looking like she is loaded and looks down to see what the problem is. By this time, he has his scepter right in front of her half turned face so that when she straightens up her nose is in the middle of it! He, meanwhile, is smiling graciously to the crowd with a look that implies that they should be patient, that the queen is mentally deranged!

On the other hand, the queen is full of her dirty tricks, too. She can step forward very quickly and pull her gown and mantle with her left hand and get the king's boots all caught up in them almost knocking him to the floor. Another little trick the queen performs is while the king is looking upstairs she sweeps her scepter savagely from her waist to one side and hits his majesty right in his royal jewels! It is amazing to watch a king in such agony smile and form the words on his lips, "You bitch! You did that on purpose!" Much of the time this foolishness goes over the audience's head, but to the true, loyal ball-goers, they are waiting for things like this and proceed to go to pieces behind their programs.

In all fairness, I should state that all Mardi Gras balls have rehearsals. Men and ladies organizations have to do this due to scenery changes, placement of officers, maids, dukes, etc. Of course, they never have full dress rehearsals but, sadly, many of the costumes are simply not finished. Some are being completed right up to the beginning of the ball. I can't tell you how many times an announcer would call for the queen of a ball to enter and just as she steps forward into the spotlight, the dressmaker is cutting the last thread in the bodice of the gown as the queen is being sewn into it. Honestly, most of the time it is not the dressmaker's fault. Kings, queens and, yes, captains could be pretty haphazard about fittings. They think, oh well, everything will be alright and for some strange reason, it usually is. All of the little and big mishaps that happen on the auditorium floor are never planned, they just seem to happen, and they seem to happen in the balls I design. But over the years, I've learned to roll with it. After all, it's Mardi Gras!

Queen, Krewe of Bal Masque 1950's

Fittings - - Where Miracles Happen
And
Balls - - Where It's Too Late for Miracles

A costume designer's prayer:

"Lord, please let my queen be pretty, good shoulders, nice bust, small waist and a wonderful personality, and may the king be tall, no belly, straight legs, sober and please let him leave his wife at home."

Larry had dozens of beautiful girls as queens and supermen as kings, but he also had his share of challenges relative to the human physique. The women he drew in costumes all looked like models from *Vogue,* but unfortunately, this didn't apply very often in the real world. I like his description of the kings. He said they were often shaped like port-o-lets, wine barrels and, occasionally, the eggplant with two toothpicks in the bottom for legs. Months later, after sweat, tears, wire, elastic, foam rubber, girdle and lifts for the boots, a very nice looking man was born. Many a wife turned to Larry the night of the ball and said, "Is that my husband, Harold? He's better looking than Paul Newman." Well, not quite but close.

Many a queen stepped into the role with the illusion that she was already the most gorgeous thing on earth, and by the last costume fitting, she was telling Larry, the dressmaker and the captain how she wanted everything done. However, some were perfect ladies throughout the entire experience.

Larry never got used to ladies using foul language, and through the years, he had quite a few. The worst of all was the previously mentioned Camilla LeDuke. She was not a pretty woman although some said when she was young she was quite beautiful. She was small, but square shaped. She was the ultimate imbiber and could out-drink ten men at a time. When she did, she got nastier and nastier.

Costumes had a way of changing entirely from a fitting to the night of the ball, and no one was more upset than Larry. One particular horror involved a group of Texans who had been lassoed into being in a ball all about Texas history. Background had nothing to do with it, but it helped that they were stinking rich. The lady captain made all kinds of wild promises that her carnival ball and night parade were bigger and better than Rex and all the others combined. She assured that the queen would be one of the city's leading citizens, very prominent and very beautiful with a French background. Well, they bought it. The lovely French beauty was none other than dear Camilla. She was to be *The Yellow Rose of Texas,* and the costume would have been stunning the way Larry designed it. The gown was of yellow velvet with a gold lace collar, entirely worked in a rose design of rhinestones and beads--very lovely. But that isn't how it turned out. Instead the costume looked like the queen represented the lush, green plains of Texas. As Larry described it:

Camilla appeared on the floor to the tune of "Yellow Rose of Texas," but she was in a brilliant emerald green, sequined sheath with a collar of more green plumes than there were ostriches! They were everywhere with several dozen at her hips as well as in her crown. I thought she looked like Big Bird on St. Patrick's Day. As I watched from upstairs in the balcony, I felt myself getting ill, the audience was howling with such laughter. Someone decided, perhaps Camilla herself that green orchids on her scepter would really top it off. They were the most nauseous shade of green, hung from every angle on her scepter and, as an afterthought to enhance her beauty she had two to the side of her crown, unfortunately, one slipped over her left eye. Her mantle was of green velvet and sequins and, to be sure, she was true to the music. In the middle of the mantle was a gigantic jeweled yellow rose, the size of a toilet seat. I wept. I would like to say that it ended there, but no, it got worse.

In those days most kings and dukes of the ladies' krewes wore the traditional black full dress suit but were just starting to wear white, full dress with white shoes and socks, so I really didn't have anything to do with their attire. This particular king, from Dallas, Texas, was short, fat and bald and looked like Boss Hog from "The Dukes of Hazard." To my dismay, he wore four inch cowboy boots of some shiny, strange looking leather. Instead of a crown, he wore a huge white 20 gallon hat completely studded with rhinestones and an emerald green sequined cape, as well as a green, wide sash across his belly fastened with a huge rhinestone star like a sheriff's badge. Someone had thoughtfully added three inch rhinestone bandings to the lapels of his jacket and down each side of his pants. But it gets better.

The king had a set of pearl-handled six shooters in jeweled holsters on each hip. No one, not even the captain, me or the audience, anticipated what he would do when his name was announced as king. He strutted out into the spotlight, smiled, bowed from the waist, pulled out his guns and let loose two shots to the ceiling. There were screams, women seated in the front floor section scattered, the band stopped playing and people ran across the floor and stage. What a disaster! Somehow, someone got to the microphone and told everyone to calm down. The band played a very shaky arrangement of "Deep in the Heart of Texas." The king was hustled to the throne by several committee men and two policemen. The house lights went up and over the roar of the crowd could be heard his majesty screaming, "What the hell's going on here? Gimme back my guns. I'm the God-damned king of Mardi Gras, you stupid bastards!" The whole time dear Camilla was doubled over in spasms of laughter, her dozens of green plumes shaking so badly, she was molting.

Queen, Krewe of Carrollton 1950's

Queen, Krewe of Elenians 1960's

Queen, Krewe of Carrollton 1960's

Who Says You Can't Turn a Sow's Ear into a Silk Purse?

I recorded Larry relating the following true story. It depicts how he, as the designer, often had to get involved with his clients and their families to prepare for a ball. Many times he worked with people who had no experience with the process. He would walk them through every step of the way until the big night. As a result, he was often thrown into personal situations that involved a lot of drama and comedy at its best and worst:

One night long ago a very fine men's ball was to have as its king a gentleman, let's call him Harold, who was not familiar at all with Mardi Gras as far as the balls went. He was, shall we say, "New Rich" or as my grandmother used to say, "A beggar on horseback." He was not a bad looking man but was tall, rumpled and a little stoop shouldered. He was balding and didn't smile but was very nice. Well, his wife really couldn't care less when he agreed to be king of this ball as neither one had ever been to one. The theme was Marco Polo with the captain portraying Marco. The king and queen would be the Emperor and Empress of China. The costumes were beautiful. The king's was scarlet, imported velvet over burnt orange silk brocade, with the long great coat over a shorter tunic underneath, tight pants and boots of gold, turned up to a point. The king looked at the sketch, puzzled, and said, "How am I gonna look like that? I ain't no Chinaman. You don't think folks will laugh at me do you?" I assured him that no one would laugh, and he would look fabulous. Fortunately, his wife was not there. It was her bingo night, and she couldn't be bothered. The king took me aside and asked me one small favor. "Would you kind of look out for my wife? I don't care what it costs, but I want her to look nice, too. Does she have to look like a Chinese lady? She's kind of blonde if you know what I mean." I had seen her and was about to tell him she had never been blonde, if he knew what I meant, but he was so darn nice I couldn't. "Would you like something designed for her or would you like me to help pick something out?" He didn't know, but she would need shoes and a purse for her cigarettes. With that he reached for his wallet, complete with rubber band around it and pulled out eight one hundred dollar bills. "Here, will this do?" He slapped them into my hands and said, "I want her to look real good, you know what I mean?" A bit surprised, I replied, "No, no, we don't do it like that." "Oh, you need more money? OK," he said. And with that he started to dip into his wallet again.

"No wait, I mean we have to start at the beginning with your wife. I have to talk to her, see what her tastes are, what she will be comfortable in, things like that," I replied. "Oh! That's easy," he said. "She likes her old ratty bathrobe, my old shirt and her tennis shoes, and even I know she can't wear that." I smiled and said, "No, Your Majesty, she can't."

Winnie, as I shall call the king's wife, was a hell of a nice lady. She really did not expect Harold's sudden wealth to change their lifestyles. They were not young but were always happy with little money. True, they sold their old house near the Fifth District Police Station and rented a lovely apartment near Audubon Park, which may have been a mistake. Uptown was simply not yet ready for them. Winnie asked the apartment rental agent why there were no clothes lines in the back yards. Somehow it all worked out. They settled in the apartment. I made an appointment for the next afternoon. The ball was four months away, but I would need every second. When I mentioned their names to the doorman at their beautiful apartment building, his eyes looked to heaven, and he simply said, "Oh, THEM!" Winnie's outfit, when she opened the door, was even more than Harold described. Her do-it-yourself blonde hair was up in several dozen hair rollers covered by a net. She wore a plaid flannel robe, that had seen better days years ago, over an oversized sweatshirt which read "Remember the Alamo, San Antonio, Texas," very patched up jeans and the largest blue furred slippers I had ever seen. She was an eyeful.

"Come on in, honey, Harold had to go to Canal Street on business. What-do-you-want-to-drink? (This was all one word.) Ignorant me. Sit down and take a load off your feet, honey. Boy, do you look swell!" I had yet to open my mouth, I just stood there gaping. "Why, thank you. It was so nice of you to see me on such short notice." She continued, "You know, honey, Harold told me you lived right down there on Louisa Street between Dauphine and Burgundy. They got some really swell old houses in those couple of blocks. What's your old man do?" I replied, "Well, my father passed away in 1949." She quickly said, "Oh, honey, I'm sorry, me and my big mouth. What I mean is, I'll bet you all ain't originally from here 'cause you talk so funny. I don't mean funny but not Ninth Ward like, you know what I mean? Well, enough of this. I got coffee and some cold Dixie in a long neck, and if you want anything stronger, we have all that other crap over at the bar. Me and Harold never was much for that other stuff, give us our good old Dixie any day."

"A Dixie will be fine," I said. "And we got cold glasses just like they do at Bud Rip's," she called back as she went to the kitchen. I looked over at the bar, and what a selection it had. There was the finest quality bourbon, scotch, gin, vodka and everything in between. There was French champagne in silver buckets and glasses for every purpose. Most still had the price tags on them.

"Nice, huh?" she said as she entered with two long neck Dixies, frosted mugs and a can of cashews. She added, "I like peanuts better myself, I like to crack the little bastards right out their shell, but Harold says this is more elegant." With that she kicked her slippers off and curled up in a chair. After she was comfortable, she looked at me and said, "Well, now ya seen me, what do you think? Not much to work with, huh?" I smiled and said, "Well, I wouldn't say that but what we have to do is find out what you'd be happy wearing. I think comfort is so important." She laughed and asked, "Can I go like this?" Fortunately, she was kidding. I talked her into going to my mother's hairstylist, got her to lose about twenty pounds and turned her over to a lady I knew at D.H. Holmes who taught her how to apply the right make-up for her coloring. I sent her to another lady who taught her that the right foundation garments would do wonders for her and give her a whole new body. Last but not least, I designed her several evening gowns and a cocktail dress or two. Her gown as the king's wife was a burnt orange silk chiffon, soft, graceful and flowing. It looked wonderful with her new ash blonde hair color touched with her own natural gray. Most people didn't recognize her. Her husband, the king, said, "I didn't know you could be so pretty." The captain's wife remarked to someone, "I didn't know she could be so graceful." Winnie said, "I didn't know I could be so uncomfortable. This damn girdle is killing me!"

The king looked fabulous and pulled off his role without a hitch. His wife, though uncomfortable, was a hit. The two were grateful and said they would remember it always, but they still went back to their old ways, being comfortable and drinking their cold Dixie beer.

Queen, Krewe of Iris 1960's

Queen 1960's

Queen, Krewe of Elenians 1960's

Queen, Krewe of Aurora 1970's

Popular Ball Themes

Larry designed hundreds of ball themes throughout his fifty year career. When New Orleans celebrated the sesquicentennial, no less than six clubs wanted it as their theme. What a year! It was a long time before he wanted to have anything to do with French period pieces. Here are highlights of his favorites:

Arabian Themes – Arabian themes were always popular for Carnival balls. *The Thief of Bagdad, The Adventures of Sinbad*, snake charmers and evil genies were all big hits with him. The costumes were colorful and exotic. So, many years later, when the captain of a ladies' or men's krewe would ask him about an Arabian theme, he would jump at the chance. Through the years he designed costumes for such themes as *The Arabian Nights, Tales from the Arabian Nights, Sinbad the Sailor, The Magic Lamp, Nights in Bagdad, Omar Khayyam's World, the Flying Carpet* and *In a Persian Palace*. Larry thought this kind of theme lent itself well to beautiful costuming. The fabrics were so rich, brocades caught the light well and chiffon and organdy moved beautifully on the floor. The theme was good for both men and women with the great robes hiding a lot of figure faults. And those great veils, that covered the bottom of a woman's face from the nose down, often were a real act of mercy. Larry recalled this theme:

> *I loved it when Sabu, in a turban and diaper, shouted, "Come my Princess, we must flee before the Caliph makes you marry the evil Prince." Then either Sabu and Maria Montez or Yvonne DeCarlo would jump on a waiting camel, either lady in sixty yards of multi-colored chiffon and enough jewelry to break the camel's back! They were followed by twenty or thirty giggling harem girls in those see-through chiffon bloomers with rubies in their belly buttons. They would all flee to an exotic desert oasis and wait for either John Hall or Douglas Fairbanks Jr. to rescue them. BUT, not before the leading lady took her bath in an Olympic sized pool filled with goat's milk. I often wondered where the hell they got all those goats! Scenes like this inspired me years later when I designed costumes with an Arabian theme. The only thing I couldn't pull off was figuring out a way for the krewe to take a bath in the middle of the auditorium in a pool filled with goat's milk.*

Princess Scherazade, Krewe of Carrollton 1970's

Peacock Princess, Krewe of Carrollton 1950's

Broadway Themes- Broadway themes were always popular for balls and parades. Larry was delighted to have designed so many through the years, like *Ziegfeld Follies,* no less than eight times. He also designed for *My Fair Lady, The King and I, Showboat, Camelot, Sunny, Roberta, Knickerbocker Holiday, Lute Song, Up in Central Park, Brigadoon, Jumbo, Annie Get Your Gun, Desert Song, Kismet, Kiss Me Kate, Oklahoma, Rose Marie, One Touch of Venus, Flower Drum Song* and *The Merry Widow*. Some of these were done three or four times by different krewes. *Camelot* was a particular favorite of his. Costume possibilities were endless when Broadway themes were used, but the music was important, too. The melodies from the shows were used to bring out the maids. Many Broadway tunes became standard official entrance pieces for captains, such as "Mame," "Hello Dolly," "That's Entertainment" and "There's No Business like Show Business." Fortunately, Larry had an extensive background in music, so designing balls about music and shows was an absolute joy. The audiences loved Broadway themes, with the familiar songs, singers, dancers, bright sets, lights and the costumes. The crowds that filled the Municipal Auditorium in the 50's and 60's went away happy. And there was comedy in some of the most unexpected places, things that were not supposed to happen but did, much to the delight of the crowd. Larry would say there were times when all was going well, then all of a sudden, once, twice and, often, three times in a night, something unplanned would happen. It was hard to be smug when a lovely young maid did a sweeping curtsy and lost her panties in the process. Or a queen missed the throne completely and fell to the floor on her butt. He never quite came to grips with an audience doubled over in laughter while they were supposed to be in awe of a beautiful costume.

Arthurian King 1960's

Maid, The Lady Diana 1960's

Duke, The Merry Widow 1960's

Maid, Fifi 1960's

Water Themes – Years ago the Krewe of Carrollton did their theme about *The Wonders of the Sea,* and it was stunning, filled with lots of color. With themes like this, Larry was always in search of fish, a shell or some sea fauna that had never been used for a ball. As beautiful as it all was, he used some unseemly creatures from the sea, too, like octopi, and sting rays. He told me of a mother whose daughter was a maid in one ball. Someone asked her what her daughter had been in the ball, and she just smiled and replied, "Oh, Charlene was an octopus." Larry also loved coral, because you could create such interesting shapes and forms with it. Seaweed and some of the shells were stunning.

He spent a lot of time at the Aquarium and in pet stores where he would sketch some of the different fish and different forms of sea life. On one occasion, he designed a particular fish costume that he called the "Winged Pear Fish." Well, some of the fish loving audience asked him where he found such a fish. When he told them he made it up, that there was no such fish, they insisted they had definitely seen pictures of this fish and wanted to buy it. He couldn't convince them. By the end of the evening they had Larry believing he had seen it before, too. Until he became a designer, the only thing he knew about fish, crabs, shrimp and oysters was that there were a lot of them eaten during Lent and on Fridays. He never designed a costume of an oyster loaf or a fried soft shell crab platter, but he thought they had definite possibilities. He did, however, have a maid once portray an oyster on the half shell. But in the long run, as Larry said, "A fish is a fish, a pearl is a pearl and an oyster on the half shell with horseradish and Tabasco is still the best with a cold Dixie beer."

This theme brings us to the notorious Camilla LeDuke once again, with Larry recounting "Venus Rising from the Sea":

A lovely ladies club decided on a sea theme and thought it would be different for the queen to represent Venus rising from the sea, somewhat like the famous painting. But I didn't count on two things, the stage that comes up from the depths of the auditorium floor or dear Camilla! The stage had never failed me. Through the years it had popped up the devil, monsters, a reviewing stand with the Mayor of the city on it, and now, as we had planned, to come up through pale blue and aqua smoke and bubbles with dear Camilla, arresting in a pink shell, as Venus. No queen had ever made an entrance quite like this. Well, neither did Camilla, not quite. On this fateful night all was going well, but Camilla was still as nasty as ever, but wasn't as loaded as usual. She even half way liked her costume, which had a great many pearls draped here and there, the colors of the sea, blues, aqua, and greens, all chiffons heavily worked in rhinestones and beads. She wore a shell crown on her black dyed curls and ostrich plumes of the sea colors. I didn't particularly want the plumes, but Camilla had a thing for anything with feathers on it. Well, the narrator finally came to the announcement that the queen was to appear. She had been preceded by the court, costumed coral, shells, sea horses, sea fern, etc. And now his voice thundered, "The Queen representing 'Venus Rising from the Sea.'" The auditorium was flooded with lime lights and music, and a group of lovely dancing girls came out as sea nymphs. Suddenly, from the dark pit of the auditorium floor, there was colored smoke and hundreds of bubbles. It was really quite dramatic. Well, as the music swelled and swelled, the call-out section was a little restless, and there was a hum upstairs in the balcony. You could see the tips of the plumes of the queen's crown, but that was all. Well, just as elevators in big office buildings often do, that's what happened to the stage elevator here. It wouldn't go up and couldn't go down. The narrator, not sensing this, once again bellowed, "The Queen as 'Venus Rising from the Sea.'" The audience started giggling, and several committee men went over to the pit trying to figure out what to do. Then, in a voice that could be heard loud and clear, Camilla yelled, "You stupid bastards get me out of here, you hear me, RIGHT NOW!" Suddenly, the hole in the floor was surrounded by committee men, firemen and two men from the crash unit of the police department. What a mess! All I could think of was, why me? Or, I should say, why me again? The captain was starting to pace back and forth from the pit to the bandstand. Finally, it was decided that a ladder would be put down into the opening in the floor. One or two committee men could go down and help the queen up, the ball would go on and we would all ignore this big hole in the floor and hope (and pray) that no one would fall in. The scene that followed was straight out of an old Mack Sennet movie or, at best, the Three Stooges. Everyone had settled down and were all waiting and watching to see what would happen next. First, after the ladder was produced, it had to be decided who would make this perilous journey. Of course, none of this was without the blood curdling screams of Camilla down below who was calling all peering down at her a stupid bunch of mother you-know-whats, and that was one of the milder expressions! The audience was delighted, shocked, and yes, some dear old girls in the call-out boxes were about to pass out with the language. I got downstairs and got the band to play some current popular music. By this time it was decided who to send down into the pit to calm and retrieve dear, old Camilla. The lucky winner proceeded down. Suddenly a head emerged with plumes and crooked crown, clutching the ladder, as twenty or so hands reached out to help her up. She looked down and back and roared, "TAKE YOUR F-ING HANDS OFF MY ASS, YOU GOD DAMN PERVERT!" Oh, what a sight! In a total state of disarray, Camilla climbed up onto the floor, her costume torn, part of it caught up in her girdle and her bodice ripped exposing more cleavage. She had the look of a wild animal that had just been captured. The crowd let out a great roar of approval, they clapped and cheered, the queen had been saved. Being the extreme show woman she was, she pulled her dress up, down, straightened her crown and, with all the dignity of a lady who had just been presented to the Queen of England, the Pope and the President, she ascended the steps to her throne, turned to the audience and with a great sweep of her scepter, acknowledged everyone in the auditorium. They loved every minute of it. One thing I'll give the lady, when she wanted to, she could be the best, but when the wind wasn't blowing her way, LOOK OUT!

Duke, The Golden Treasures of King Neptune, Krewe of Carrollton 1960's

Duke escorting maid, Carrollton 1960's

The "Old South" Themes – Larry designed many patriotic themes through the years. But he also designed dozens about the glories of the Confederacy. The audiences loved themes about the "Old South" complete with ladies in hoop skirts with fans or parasols. Through the years he designed *The South before the Civil War, The Old South, The Glories of the South, A Plantation Party, The Beauties of the South* and a personal favorite of his, *Bride of Fortune*. When the orchestra in the auditorium played "Dixie," the crowd went crazy, and they usually stood all the way to the last row upstairs. However, women couldn't gracefully handle the hoop skirts and all those petticoats. It was one thing to walk in them, but seven out of ten had never mastered the art of sitting down in a hoop skirt. It is clear why they wore pantaloons in the old days.

As pretty as the gowns were for these southern themes and for "Spring Fiesta," a social event that took place in New Orleans every spring, they were really much more trouble than they were worth to him, as a designer, and a real headache to the dressmaker. Yards and yards of fabric had to be sewn with sequined braids, lace and rhinestones, back, front and sides. One year the queen of one club was so tiny, and there was so much dress, that she simply couldn't wield it. However, two veteran committee men walked on either side of her, not only guiding her, but ever-so discretely and gently with their gloved hands, easing the hoop and petticoat up so most of the strain was lifted from her. She looked as if she was effortlessly gliding along as if on ice.

Maid, early 1950's

Maid, 1970's

Opera Themes – As a teenager Larry was one of the lucky students who ushered at the New Orleans Municipal Auditorium for all the big operas. It was his passion and his favorite theme to design, so he was thrilled when asked to design a complete opera theme for a men's club. Knowing little about opera, the captain told Larry to pick out what he thought would be the prettiest for the court, himself, the king and the queen. This was a designer's dream come true. Larry had many wonderful books on operas, and he had kept every opera program as souvenirs. Where to start? Which ones? *Carmen, La Traviata, Madame Butterfly, Romeo & Juliet, Sampson & Delilah, Tales of Hoffman, Aida* and *Faust* were all exquisitely represented in the end. For the captain, he chose Mephistopheles from *Faust*. In later years he would use him, Satan, and the King of the Underworld many times, because he could make such colorful and dramatic costumes for those characters. This particular ball worked out beautifully, and he was so proud.

Fate was not always kind when later designing more opera themes. Some were as beautiful as the first one and others were disasters--everything went wrong, the audience howled, and Larry thought he set opera back one hundred years. The costumes were fine, but the people and situations were beyond belief. Over the years he had many an oversized Madame Butterfly, an Escamillo or two from *Carmen* who were shaped like Curley of the *Three Stooges*, and a Sampson that brought tears to his eyes. This theme story was comically told by Larry:

One year a captain, a music lover, decided it would be very dramatic if the maid and duke, portraying the characters in the opera, would mouth the arias with the real stars of the opera on record, like lip syncing. What a mess! It was straight out of A Night at the Opera with the Marx Brothers, only funnier. The thing that made it so horrible was that those taking part in it had never been to an opera, didn't like opera and couldn't have cared less. One of the unforgettable moments of this mess was while poor Marguerite sang the jewel song from Faust to Mephistopheles (the devil) she stepped on his tail (how he ever got a tail was a mystery to me) which came off much to the delight of the audience! On the other hand, the poor young girl lip syncing the "Habanera" from Carmen got so excited she hit her poor duke, Don Jose, with her fan and his mustache came off. All he did was giggle--he was so loaded he didn't care.

I had no better luck with a large Madame Butterfly who got her umbrella caught in her wig, and while struggling with her umbrella and kimono, big foot Lt. Pinkerton, trying to help, stepped on her costume and nearly knocked her flat on her rear. By this time the audience wasn't even trying to hide their laughter, they were just enjoying the whole thing. But his agony wasn't over yet. Enter Sampson and Delilah. He was a big Italian man about sixty, shaped like a wine barrel. Even worse, his arms were out (my fault) and were covered with tattoos. It was awful! They were trying to mouth out this beautiful love song from the second act, and Delilah, who was supposed to be very sensual and loaded with passion, looked more like Twiggy and was as skinny as a pipe cleaner.

Later, I had Juliets, who looked like Dolly Parton, Toscas weighing in at 185 pounds and a duke, playing Othello, who was a Moor and supposed to be dark, but the makeup man got carried away, and he ended up looking like Bill Robinson in an old Shirley Temple movie. To those who were great opera lovers, I may have been a disgrace. To the poor costume designer, these events were disastrous. But, one old lady told me later, "The balls you design are worth putting a girdle on for, honey." I took her remark as a compliment.

Maid, Camelot 1960's

Captain, Krewe of Naiads, 1960's

Duke, The Fortune Teller, Krewe of Virgilians 1960's

Maid, The Fortune Teller, Krewe of Virgilians 1960's

Melody Themes – One theme Larry never got tired of was songs, popular songs, old songs, pop or classical. He loved songs that went with color, like "Deep Purple," "Red Sails in the Sunset," "Tangerine," and "Daybreak." Most captains preferred their sweet young maids in something full, pretty and romantic. But if the song was appropriate, like "Jealousy" or "Temptation," and the maid had a good figure, Larry would put her in a slinky, sexy costume. The audience would whisper behind their programs, "How does she keep it on?" "Do you suppose she has anything on under there?" "What do you suppose will happen when she curtsies?" They never said that about a man in costume. These costumes didn't make any points with the ladies in the call-out section. Larry always felt that if you were blessed with a beautiful body, show it! He wanted his designs to make a statement, and they did. One night after a ball about songs, one pure as snow old lady said of one of the maids, "I always thought that song was pretty till he (meaning Larry) got hold of it. Now I think it's nasty."

Looking back, Larry wasn't out to do a sweet ball. Costumes, in the early days, were somewhat dull as far as color, style and originality. Use of color and beading were two things Larry was known for. He used certain kinds of beads and rhinestones to capture just the right effects with the colors of the costumes and the lighting. However, he created quite a few white gowns for debutantes in his day. Although they looked traditional, on closer inspection there was something very different about them, a little touch that set them apart. One disgruntled society matron, upon learning her daughter had not received a bid to be queen of an old line club but only a maid, told him, "Now I don't want her dress to be prettier than the queen's. That would be in bad taste, but I do want them to know that Mitsy is on the floor." Well, her dress was stunning. It was full and pretty and when she moved, inside the imported French lace design were dozens and dozens of rhinestones and pin-head sized sequins that glittered ever so brilliantly when caught by the light. She made her point. She was the prettiest girl out there and made the queen look very overdone, overdressed and overweight. It goes without saying that the queen's momma never spoke to Larry's client again.

Maid, Fascination, Krewe of Iris early 1970's

Magnolias and Other Flower Themes – The following is Larry's description of this theme:

I started drawing magnolias in City Park as a child when I attended children's art classes at Delgado Museum from the time I was eight until twelve years old. My dad would bring me early on Saturday mornings. I was so excited I was ready at 7:00 am. I told my parents all the great things I would draw or paint that day, and it didn't matter if it rained either. On good days we sketched all over the park. On rainy and cold days we sketched inside the damp, spooky museum. Sometimes Miss Bathernem, our teacher, gave us a talk in the many art chambers of how this or that artist started, what he liked to paint best, what part of the world he lived in, etc. I worked in all mediums and got pretty good at clay modeling and won a first prize when I was about ten years old. The other kids did vases, flower pots, ash trays and lumpy heads. I did a magnolia and a mermaid on a rock combing her hair. She had a beautiful body, was bare breasted and was wrapped around a rock. For my age I guess it was quite erotic, but I had drawn nudes in the museum two years prior, so it seemed natural to me.

For the show in the museum, where all work was displayed, the mermaid stood out from the rest. My father thought the magnolia was better. Of course, some of the other parents thought I was a little too advanced for my age. My parents were so proud when I won the first prize blue ribbon and a twenty five dollar gift certificate to a local art store. So for many years before I became a designer, I painted magnolias, many of them, both in watercolor and oil. When I got the chance to do them in costumes, I really felt I knew as much about them as anyone. I used them in both men's and ladies' balls, on captains, maids, dukes and once as a design for a mantle. I thought the magnolia was a great flower to work with, because it was pretty, large and you saw what it was right away. Some flowers, no matter how much you exaggerated them, never looked right. Violets, sweet peas, and any small blossomed flower were difficult on certain fabric. Through the years I've used every kind of flower and made up a few along the way.

In one ball years ago, I made up the exotic 'Blue Rose of Mars' and the 'Deadly Moon Lily.' Some flower themes were, The Enchanted Garden, Flowers of Love, Gardens of the Old South, Tinkerbelle's Secret Garden, Flowers of the World, the Beauty of Roses, Gardens in the Moonlight and on and on.

Officer, Krewe of Iris 1950's

Queens without Crowns

Occasionally Larry had problems with a ball theme. There had always been a king or queen for every krewe he designed. However, historical characters could be difficult. Over the years he had to design costumes representing various characters like Variena Howel Davis, wife of Jefferson Davis, when *Bride of Fortune*, a wonderful book by local author, Harnett Kane, was the theme. Kane stated that he was flattered that his book was being done, a wonderful Civil War epic, but it was out of the question that Jefferson Davis would wear tights or a crown, or that his wife, as the wife of the President of the Confederacy, would ever wear a crown, a collar or mantle, because she was definitely not a queen. Larry loved being authentic, so instead she wore a very tiny tiara and snood, and her antebellum gown swept into a kind of mantle.

The same thing applied when another club did *The History of America*, and the king was George Washington and the queen his wife, Martha. There was no royalty in America, although the costumes of that period were much more elegant than those during the time of Jefferson Davis.

One year a smaller club decided on *Salute the Wild, Wild West* as their theme. There was no way Larry could make Wild Bill Hickock a king, and as for Annie Oakley, a queen with lace collar and crown, forget it! He dressed Wild Bill in an elaborate western costume. Chances are he would have worn something like that anyway, but instead of a crown, Larry had him wear the white, shoulder length wig, beard and mustache and carry a jeweled cowboy hat which he used instead of a scepter. He put Annie in a period gown of the Victorian age with a long, long train, a court gown as they called it. He placed jeweled symbols of the old west all over it, and she wore a very small tiara accentuated with many plumes. They both looked great.

The king from *The King and I* worked out beautifully. He wore a Siamese crown, very authentic, but no mantle. There again, Anna was definitely not royalty, so Larry dressed her as he had seen her on Broadway years before and in the movie. She wore a jeweled snood, and her gown was much more elaborate, her full skirted gown sweeping into a form of mantle. This queen loved it because she didn't want to be like other queens anyway.

Larry was unsuccessful in convincing one captain that as charming as the idea of *Great Ladies of the Theatre* was for a theme, Lillian Russell could not be a queen. She had an image and could not wear a crown, collar or mantle. From the time that the beautiful Alice Faye portrayed her on the screen, people saw her a certain way--the giant plumed hat, the trumpet lined gown and the jeweled staff. The gown could be very stunning with all the rhinestones and beadwork on it. The mantle coming from the back of her gown was gorgeous. The woman who was queen was a beautiful blonde who had an hour glass figure, perfect for the gown. Larry once jokingly said that he was very glad that some of his queens had hour glass figures, but with many of them, all of the sand had gone to the bottom. This queen's king was Diamond Jim Brady, and there was no way Larry could put him in tunic and tights. He took a chance and put him in a white, full dress suit and white top hat and vest with diamonds all over it. It worked quite nicely.

With Larry's queens of movies and Broadway, he was able to tell their stories in their mantles. He created queens of the moon, sun, heaven, hell, night, ballet and future (that one was really a challenge). One theme close to his heart was an art gallery. He dressed the maids and dukes like paintings (a piece of cake for a costume designer) and the king and queen were the *Magic of Color*. Each of their mantles was a jeweled artist pallet at the top flowing down into all of the colors an artist uses. It was extremely effective and from upstairs in the auditorium, looked quite beautiful.

On several occasions, he had queens of the *Big Top* and other circus themes. He was tempted to have his circus queen come out riding sidesaddle on a great white horse, but remembered the disaster of the Civil War ball where the horses dropped large presents all over the auditorium floor, so he thought better of it.

Duke, early 1950's

Maid, early 1950's

Grand Entrances

All captains, male or female, want two things, to have a costume like no other in the history of Mardi Gras and to make a spectacular entrance. Larry's captains were never content to simply walk down the middle of the auditorium floor, find the center spotlight and acknowledge the applause of the crowd. Through the years, he had captains come out from under the auditorium floor as devils, bats, fiery flames, Attila the Hun and the evils of the underworld, to name a few. Conversely, others descended as hope, love, birds, etc. Some captains descended from the tops of those big, red curtains and even higher depicting the sun, moon, spirit of the rainbow, rain and shooting stars, not to mention, spacemen, spacewomen, Peter Pan and more. From under the sea, he had Neptune and queens pop out of oyster shells as pearls. Let's not forget Easter eggs, magic boxes, enchanted trees and one lovely lady who came out of an engagement ring box as a diamond.

One year, the captain of Carrollton flew down from the ceiling of the auditorium at breakneck speed on a wire over a screaming and terrified audience, his arms outstretched and cape flying behind him. He went through those big red house curtains only to emerge seconds later from his wild ride none the worse for wear. The audience loved it. It wasn't until much later that it was revealed that he had a dummy dressed exactly like him, down to the last detail, who actually did the flying. His entrance was the talk of Mardi Gras for weeks.

Another year, captain of the Krewe of Sparta was a jeweled spider caught up in a giant web. He crawled down a huge net. It looked terrific. Years later Larry wrote a ball for this same captain called *The Sweetest Ball of All*. The whole court was candy, and this captain emerged from a huge Cracker Jack box as the prize. He had the Cracker Jack people put the krewe favors that year in real boxes of Cracker Jack. Later in a ball with the unlikely title of *Fortune's Fickle Fancies*, he emerged from a gigantic slot machine as the glittering "Silver Jack Pot."

Actually, the captains who did those outrageous things were the least likely ever to do so. They were, for the most part, quiet, very conservative, low keyed people, but not on the night of their ball! Other captains came out on horses (disastrous), elephants, in convertibles, vintage cars, rickshaws, boats, litters carried by slaves, Santa's sleigh pulled by cute young women dressed like reindeer or Christmas gifts and more. In addition, some came out in a sea of bubbles and in fog, rain and snow. Larry even toyed with the idea of a captain, of whom he wasn't too fond, to come out of a huge pot of real boiling water as a lobster, but decided against it since the water would ruin the sequins.

Duke, Jackpot, Krewe of Sparta 1950's

Duke, Toyland, Krewe of Carrollton 1950's

She's Gonna be Queen of the Mardi What?

Larry dealt with hundreds of Mardi Gras queens throughout his long career as a designer. Here is a story he told me about one such larger-than-life character:

Anytime a lady captain invites me to meet her for lunch, before I design the queen's gown in early summer, throws up a red flag. Awaiting the captain's arrival in Brennan's patio that beautiful summer day, I felt content and happy as I sat sipping a cold, tropical cocktail. Then the captain rushed in, one of my favorite lady captains, a no-nonsense lady. We had already decided to do "My Old Kentucky Home" with southern belles, hoop skirts, and the whole "Gone with the Wind" package. She sat down, gave me a big hug and told the waiter to bring her a double vodka martini, easy on the vermouth. "Well darling," I said, "It's got to be pretty bad for you to be drinking martinis down this time of day. What's the problem? The queen's got two heads?" "Now Youngblood, it will be alright, I don't want you to panic when you see the queen." "I'm sure I can handle it," I said. Her drink came. "Is she big?" I asked. She swallowed half her drink. "Is she big and short?" She gulped the rest and called the waiter. "Young man, bring me another and keep the damn olive out!" she said. I was beginning to feel real fear. I told the waiter, "Make that two. I feel I'm gonna need more than a drink with an umbrella in it!" Suddenly there was a roar of confusion in the carriage way that led to both the dining room and the patio, and a loud voice with the most horrible drawl I had ever heard announced to the restaurant manager, "I'm the new Queen of the Mardi Gras! Tell Mrs. Martha Waters (not her real name) and ma costume designer ah have arrived." Well, heads turned, drinks stopped in mid-air and forks never reached the customers' mouths.

Standing there in the bright sunlight was not the Queen of Mardi Gras, but indeed, something that resembled one of the floats! She was over sixty, very short and plump. Yes, I am being kind. Her waist was cinched; she had a huge rear, big hips and skinny legs. Her hair, which she was to tell us later was frosted apricot, was done especially for her in Alabama, looked electrocuted and was very, very frizzy. She used make-up extravagantly, had two bright pink rouge circles on her cheeks. I had never seen skin so white. For color, she added the "Cleopatra look" over her beady little eyes. Her scarlet Cupie doll lips were a tribute to Clara Bow of the 1920's. Her wide brimmed hat was of palest blue and to one side of her face was the biggest, bluest, silk cabbage rose I had ever seen. Her dress was a mass of blue organdy ruffles (shades of a senior prom) and was full. Her belt, as her bag, was of some strange reptile skin. She wore pale blue lace stockings and three inch, ankle strap navy sandals. I will say here and now, I have never seen anything like it in my life, except perhaps a drag queen on Mardi Gras day, but he was in pink! So far, I have only described the mere trifles, let's get to the big stuff (not her size).

For jewelry, it appeared she had rhinestone clusters hanging from her ears. A slim gold chain with a diamond the size of a grape was around her neck. On every finger, except her thumbs, were a mass of square cut, pear shaped and odd shaped diamonds, rubies and an occasional emerald, all fake, I thought! She explained later that they were all real. "Hector, my late husband just loved to give his little sweet potato little trinkets all the time. I used to say to him, 'Sugar Man, you are spoiling little ole me just rotten!' But it seemed to make him so happy." A real tear made its way down her powdered cheek and she produced a blue, sheer lace trimmed handkerchief that must have lain in the bottom of a perfume vat for years. WOW! I suddenly felt tears in my eyes, not from sympathy, but from the damn perfume!

We were seated right in the main dining room where we could be seen by everyone, just our luck. A real appetite breaker! One waiter approached (I think they drew straws) and asked, "May I bring you a drink?" She quickly and loudly replied, "Ya bet your sweet little ass, honey! I'll have Jack Daniels on the rocks with a beer chaser, and they'll have whateva they're drinking." Martha and I quickly ordered double vodka martinis and I told the waiter to HURRY! The queen followed up with, "Ah don't know how you people can drink that nasty ole vodka. You all know it's made from rotten ole potato drippings, one hundred percent alcohol, and ah don't know what all! I oughta know, honey, cause my granddaddy drank about three fifths of it a day. He lived to be ninety seven years old. We didn't even have to embalm him. He was already pickled!" With that she shrieked and roared, "That's a joke darling, I used that to tell ma husband, Sugar Man, and he nearly died laughing!" I looked at the captain with panic, but her only reply was, "Waiter, bring us two more double martinis RIGHT AWAY!" I was pretty close to dying myself.

Maid, Betsy Ross 1960's

Maid, Lady in Waiting to Maria Theresa of Spain

Darryl and Edna

The following situation greatly disturbed Larry, but he kept it to himself putting it to paper so that years later he would not forget any details. Later he told me the story, definitely worth sharing, told as only Larry could:

No one was surprised when Darryl married Edna. She was exactly what he had been looking for. She was very, very rich, and she was at least twenty years older than he. Darryl was handsome, if you liked a man slim, who moved like a dancer, which, in fact, he had been when he was younger. He was maitre de at one of the city's rather posh restaurants when Edna met him. Of course, she was immediately attracted to Darryl. Everyone loved him. He was the answer to every widow and old and rich divorcee's prayers. He remembered all names, what they liked to drink and eat and where they liked to sit. He was extravagant with flattery and made most of the old gals feel young again.

Poor Edna was as smitten as a teenager. She took to dying her already bleached hair to a shade of pink. It was very colorful. She had a head full of frizzy pink into blonde into gray curls. She was over made-up and overdressed at all times.

Everyone was happy when they did slip down to St. Bernard Parish and were married. She had been widowed fifteen years earlier and her husband had left her a bundle plus a stunning home on St. Charles Avenue. Darryl, on the other hand, had never been married and, judging from the group he was seen with occasionally in the French Quarter, he didn't seem like the type who would. Well, they were seen everywhere together. They went to the opera, the symphony and all the big charitable, formal affairs. He left his job, naturally, and where as they still went to the restaurant, they usually entertained at their home on "the Avenue." Their pictures were seen in the society pages very often.

Finally, Edna was approached to be queen of one of the ladies' krewes. She was thrilled and, of course, nothing would do but her husband, Darryl, to be her king. Edna really did take the Duchess of Windsor's advice seriously--"You couldn't be too thin or too rich." The poor lady was skin over bone and, in the last few years, had a few face lifts plus a nip and tuck. Darryl, on the other hand, seemed to look younger and younger, and free of his tuxedo from his former job showed a grand flare for color but in a classy way.

I had known Edna for a few years, but didn't know how to make a pipe cleaner with pink hair look good. But Darryl was so interested in every inch of her costume, every bead, every sequin, the way it fit, and he asked a million questions. Would her heels be the right size? Would a wig be better for the crown rather than her own hair? He even bought her a foundation which already came equipped with a set of falsies and a padded rear end. Through it all, the fittings and everything else, Edna was in heaven. Her man, as she had taken to calling him, wanted her to look like Lana Turner. The dressmaker and I looked at each other knowing that the only way she would have of ever looking remotely like Lana Turner would be if God chose this moment to perform a spectacular miracle. He didn't, of course.

Darryl didn't have to worry about a costume for himself, because in those days, the king and dukes wore a black full dress suit. This was long before the ladies started putting dukes in costumes to match theirs. The day of the ball arrived, and so far it all looked pretty normal. There was the usual hectic rehearsal at the auditorium with the band, light sets, narrator and entertainers; however, the king was notably absent. The husband of one officer took his place. No one seemed to think too much of it but me, so I wandered to the back of the stage where the dressing rooms were. I already knew what I would find. I opened the door gently to the queen's room, and there was Darryl in all his splendor. He had carefully slipped into the queen's gown, wig and crown and was standing in front of a triple full length mirror making 'cooing' noises at his image. I shut the door behind me. He didn't even look surprised or startled. "Well now, Larry baby, this is how it should look, don't you think?" He said this as he arranged the crown. "That wrinkled old bitch could never look this beautiful. Oh why couldn't I wear it? The right make-up, the mask, it could be done." He turned and walked over to the dressing table. He was wearing white satin pumps with three inch heels! I had to sit down before I fell down. Darryl, what the hell are you thinking of?" Darryl put a long cigarette to his lips, lit it and looked back at his reflection once again in the mirror. "But what about you, you're the king, how do we explain your no-show?" I asked but then realized, what I was saying. This was the most insane situation I had ever been in, and I didn't want any part of it! I got up to leave. He turned around and screamed, "You're the big man in Mardi Gras. Didn't you say 'Dare to be different?' Wasn't it you who put kings and queens in red, black, green and chartreuse costumes? You introduced practically bare breasts and bellies and even had the queen brought out by a bunch of half naked black men! You are going to love this, its right up your alley. It is different and I'm gonna go for it, what do you think of that?" "Not much darling, not much," Edna said very calmly. Neither of us heard her come into the room. I looked at her, she looked at Darryl and he looked at me. Then there was the most deadly silence.

Edna asked me very calmly, "Would you please leave us alone, Mr. Youngblood?" I gladly and quickly left the dressing room very shaken. I don't know what happened; I didn't say a word to anyone. I went home, took three shots of Jack Daniels, a shower, put on my full dress suit and went back to the auditorium. I had no idea what I would find when I got there. There was the usual excitement always present before a ball. I knocked on the captain's dressing room door, and it was filled with happy people toasting the captain with champagne. I asked her if everything was OK. She gave me a kiss and said, "It's going to be the most different ball yet!" My heart skipped a beat as I wondered what she meant by that.

Well, after two glasses of champagne, I went upstairs to watch this ongoing disaster. But when the time came, the queen made her entrance and looked stunning. Yes, it was Edna, and with the king's entrance, Darryl looked handsome and so proud of his wife who never did look like Lana Turner. To this day, I don't know what happened in that dressing room when I left. The ball, as well as the supper dance was wonderful. Weeks later I heard Edna and Darryl went to Europe. I never, ever told anyone what went on that night.

As the years passed, Edna and Darryl were seen here and there and seemed to be very happy. He started to gain weight and they both drank too much. Later Darryl died, and Edna took a young artist from the Quarter under her wing and helped with his career. He was about twenty-five years younger than she, and once said, "Don't you think my lady looks like Lana Turner?" I heard a wild rumor that Darryl was laid out in Edna's queen gown, but I don't believe it. Well, I don't know, you never can tell. He sure loved that costume!

Maid, Russian Doll, Krewe of Naiads 1970's

Maid, Krewe of Naiads 1950's

Costumes, Capes, Trains and Mantles

After 1965, Larry lost count of how many costumes he designed, there were so many. However, at his peak, he did have one year where 5,000 designs were created consisting of both the working and final sketches. It is interesting to note how the figures in Larry's sketches changed in style through the years from somewhat small and stiff to graceful and curvaceous to large and oversized. But over time, dozens of sketches were lost, thrown away or destroyed.

One lady captain told him that her dressmaker, originally from England, decided after twenty five years to go back home. She took all of the sketches Larry designed for the captain's krewe with her, all twenty five years worth of them! But there are people who keep every single carnival memento from their ball night and their parade. One king, who had been king of several ladies' krewes and one men's krewe, kept the costumes on mannequins completely intact inside huge glass cases. Wigs, crowns, boots, scepters, the whole thing, plus every sketch, every program and every krewe favor. It was quite impressive.

Although today there are fine fabrics that can stretch and come in amazing colors great for costumes, Larry was partial to what he called "pure" fabrics. These have few, if any, chemicals or preservatives in them. The color stays more vibrant longer and is more fade resistant. I have some of his working sketches from the 1950's with fabric swatches still pinned to them that look as new as the day they were placed there. Fabrics of good quality were not cheap then and certainly not now. Few people realize how much these costumes are worth in design, time, effort and material, not to mention the number of people involved in getting each one on the ballroom floor or on a float in a parade. In Larry's day, for one king to make an entrance, it usually took about 20-30 people, costume designers, and dressmakers and their helpers, working off and on the whole year.

During Mardi Gras, capes are worn by the captains, dukes, officers and riding lieutenants. The captain's cape is always the most beautiful, usually trimmed in velvet, white fur and worked heavily in rhinestones and sequins. In many clubs, the capes are used over and over again. But in the clubs for which Larry designed, capes were new every year.

Trains had intricate, often raised, details in the designs. However, this also meant added weight. The average train could be 12-16 feet long and weigh up to 35 pounds. This was a challenge for some ladies, especially the tiny ones. After a lot of thought and research, Larry took the advice of an engineer who suggested sewing small skate wheels underneath the edge of the train on a kind of track. When the maid or queen turned, so did the train. It worked beautifully.

In night parades, you can get away with more since the crowds' visibility is limited. However, in a daytime parade, with the bright sunshine everything can be seen, everything that is beautiful, every mistake, every thread out of place.

In the 50's and 60's the clubs for whom Larry designed had their dukes ride in open convertibles. But they, like everyone else, wanted to throw things, especially doubloons. This was a challenge, because the crowd, while trying to grab beads and doubloons, would often grab the cape. Not only was this dangerous, but the costume and cape could be damaged and the duke potentially injured. Larry often rode in the captain's convertible, spending most of the parade jumping in and out of the car arranging the captain's cape so it would be beautiful at all times. . . WHAT A MISTAKE! The crowd thought Larry had doubloons or beads for them, and when they discovered he didn't, they wanted to throw him under the car!

What happened to all those beautiful capes, trains and mantles, as well as the elaborate costumes of kings, queens, officers and so on? Some were sold to other krewes around Louisiana for their parades. Some of the krewes, both men's and ladies' organizations, kept them, as some entire balls were staged several times as entertainment at conventions and for private functions. Some made their way to the Cabildo Museum and the Costume Room at the Mint. So many were, and probably still are, simply put in a big box stored in an attic or hung in a plastic bag in some store room. Larry saw some of his works thrown in a heap at local flea markets. On one occasion, he went to a friend's house and there was the granddaughter playing "Mardi Gras Queen" in the back yard with her friends, as she trailed around in her grandmother's $2,000 (at the time) gown in the grass and dirt, dragging something that was once not only costly, but very beautiful.

Duke, China 1960's

Maid, Krewe of Iris 1960's

Duke, Shades of Purple, Krewe of Sparta 1950's

Train, The Four Seasons

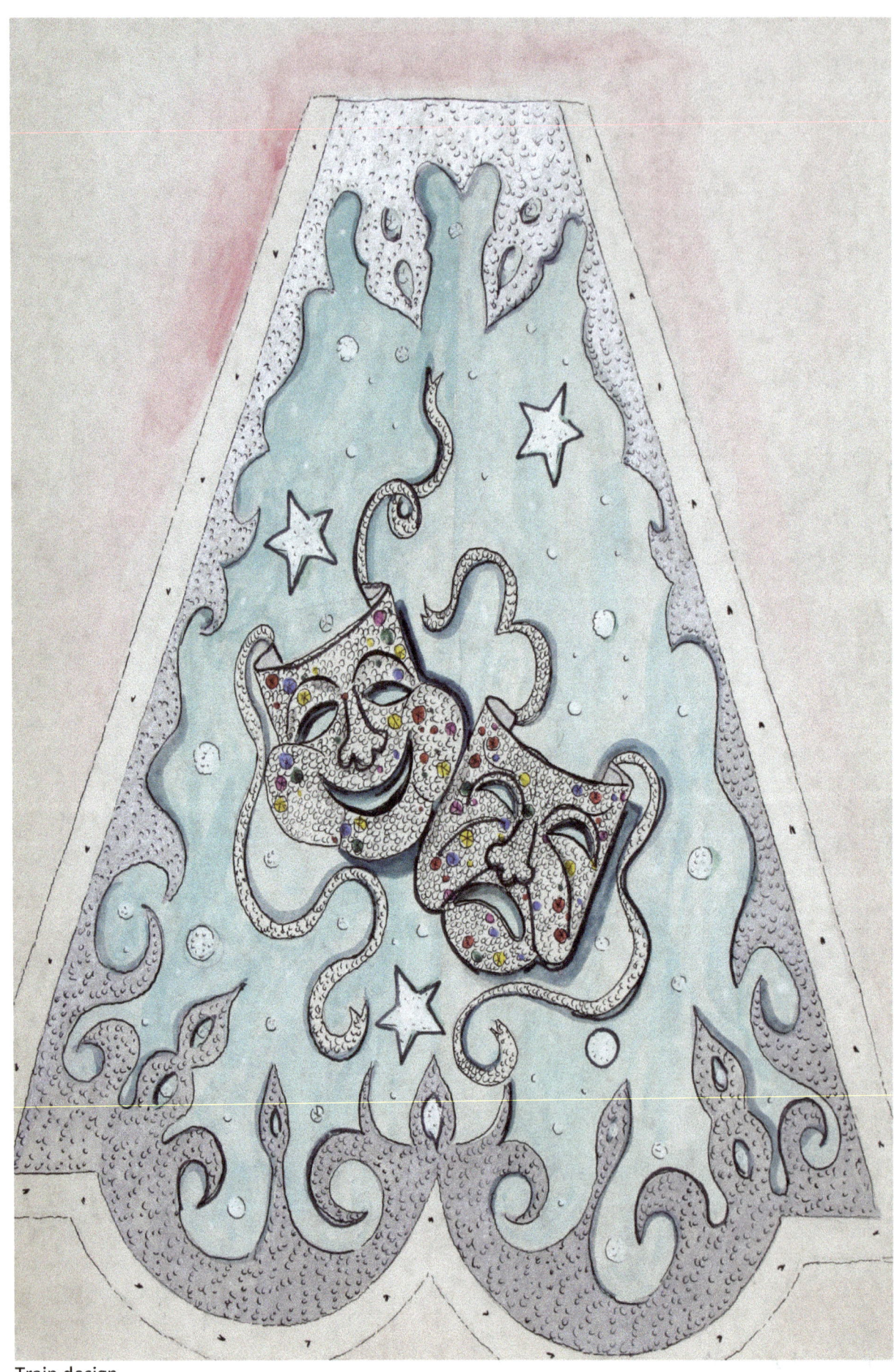

Train design

Captain, Krewe of Iris 1960's

The Adorable Little Pages (Not Really)

Pages were a real sore spot with Larry. He would have preferred the distinguished committee men, dressed in their tuxedos, assisting the kings and queens. The pages were a supreme pain to both the king and queen (unless they were their children), a headache to the captain and a nightmare to the costume designer. In many cases they were too young and unable to do their jobs well, mainly keeping the mantles straight during the Grand March and while the royal couple sat on their thrones. Afterwards, they were to sit on their little stools and behave. Instead, they often cried, screamed, wouldn't come out, walked on the mantles, waved and picked their noses, pulled on their tights and any number of things that made Larry furious. It was frustrating for him, because so much time and effort was put into a sketch; the dressmaker worked her fingers off, as did the headpiece maker, along with so many others, only to have the moment stolen. But sometimes the pages would win the hearts of the audience, stealing the lime-light from the queen and king.

Naturally, captains had a reserve of seasoned committee men who were ready to assist and, yes, in some cases, to carry off a screaming page who announced to the whole auditorium, "I gotta potty!"

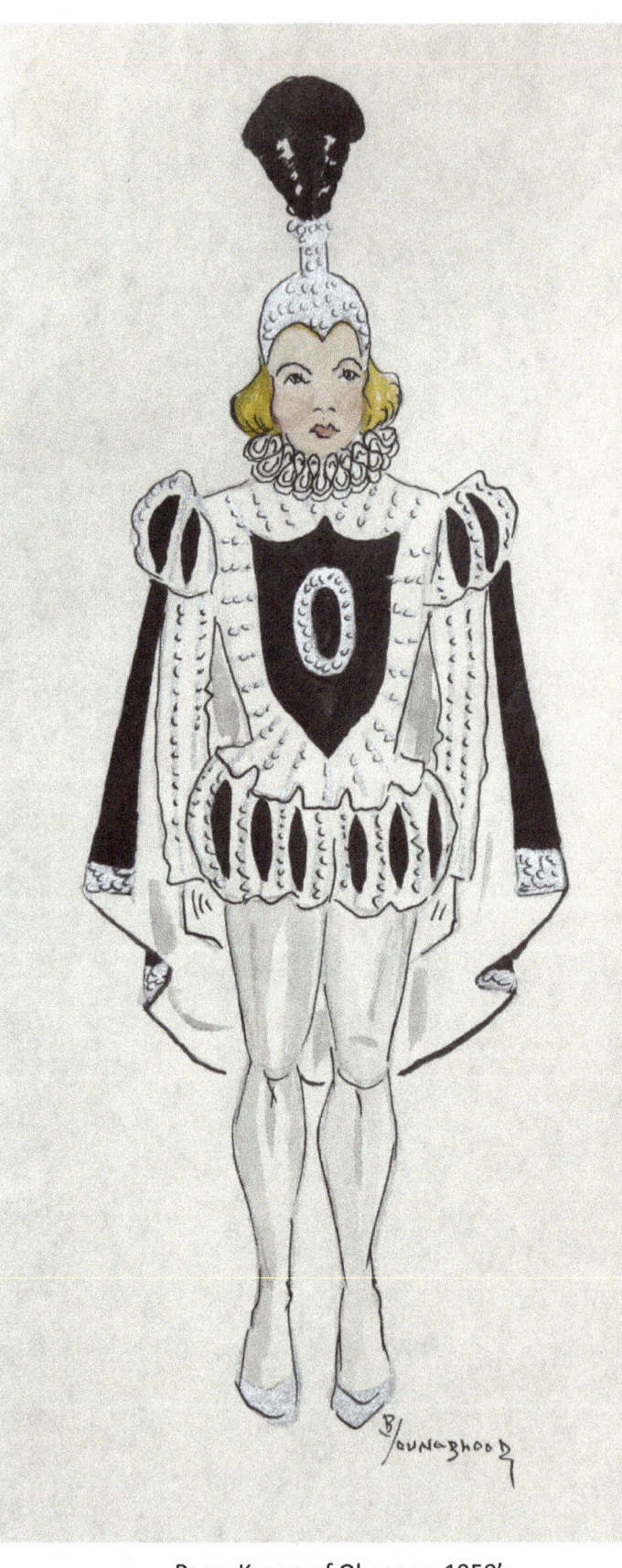

Page, Krewe of Okeanos, 1950's

The Queen Who Looked as Young as Her Daughter

Larry couldn't count the times he found himself in the middle of an awkward situation in both his personal and professional life. As you have read, some situations were unbelievable and some came complete with award-winning performances from krewe members, or in this case, one krewe's queen. Larry tells the following story:

One year in the early 50's, a ladies' krewe decided to do "Great Ladies of America." The ladies were mostly "over the hill" but were a really nice group of merry matrons. The captain, a lady who knew her way around Mardi Gras, picked the ladies who would wear each costume. Well now, Martha Washington was plump, Mary Todd Lincoln looked much like the real one, Dolly Madison, unfortunately, when she did appear in the ball, got mixed up and thought she was "Hello Dolly," Edith Wilson, old Woodrow's wife, was in real life very elegant, but somehow, this one looked more like Gypsy Rose Lee! The lady who portrayed Eleanor Roosevelt made the real one look like Liz Taylor. This should tell you how things were going. The queen was to be the greatest lady in the land, the Statue of Liberty.

However, the queen was a pleasant surprise, a very nice looking woman about forty five or fifty, good figure, small waist and a cute fanny to boot. When I met her to see the sketches, she had her daughter with her who was a carbon copy of her, only about nineteen or twenty. They looked like sisters, and I knew that they could probably wear each other's clothes. I thought nothing of that at the time. She, of course, loved the costume and her daughter was very excited.

As the fittings progressed, she would gush, "Oh Mommy, do you think I'll ever get a chance to wear anything like that?" The dressmaker, who was pinning the back of the bodice, said, "Honey, I'll bet you could probably put this on and it would fit you like a glove, right Youngblood?" I smiled as I looked at them in the three-way mirrors, laughed and said, "You're right about that." And I should have caught it then, that look, the secret smile between mother and daughter. As I've said before, most of the maids were over forty and then some. The queen's two sisters-in-law were maids also, and there was no love lost between them. They were, unfortunately, portraying Martha Washington and Mary Todd Lincoln. Little did I realize at the time that I was smack dab in the middle of a grade-A Italian vendetta. The night of the ball, everything was in its usual chaotic state, when suddenly about twenty minutes before the ball was to start, I was out front chatting with some guests when a security guard told me that the captain wanted to see me backstage right away. That always sends a chill up a designer's spine. The captain, all dressed and looking beautiful as "American Music," was in a highly emotional state. "Oh, Larry what a mess we're in, I mean big trouble!"

We went to the queen's room where lying on a sofa looking completely stunning was the queen in her robe. She was dabbing at her eyes with a dainty, lace handkerchief, being very careful not to mess up her make-up, I might add-- all very dramatic. She was surrounded by two maids, a hairdresser and her beautiful daughter. "Oh, I feel so terrible, I think that I am going to faint. My legs simply won't hold me up, I CAN'T GO ON!" Right out of a movie! But no, this was Mardi Gras in New Orleans 1954. The captain roared, "Can't go on, CAN'T GO ON? What the hell do I tell all those people out there? Come on, honey, you've just got a bad case of nerves. You'll be fine. Tell her, Youngblood, she'll be fine." "You'll be fine," I echoed. Her gown hung shimmering on the rack, imported white velvet, worked in hundreds and hundreds of rhinestones and beads. Her red, white and blue mantle draped from another sofa and her crown of jeweled spikes a la Statue of Liberty sat on a chair with her scepter, a jeweled torch of amber and ruby stones so real it looked as though it was on fire. It was all perfect, but no one to wear them, or so it seemed.

The beautiful daughter knelt at her mother's feet. "Oh, Mommy, don't cry. If you're sick, you mustn't go out there." The captain yelled, "Son of a bitch, this is a total disaster if I ever saw one!" I felt like I was in the middle of a great drama of the silver screen or Broadway at its worst, I couldn't be sure. It was eerie, but as sure as I was standing there, I knew exactly what was going to happen next. I was awe struck as I watched.

The daughter got up and stood in front of the sparkling gown running her fingers over it. She turned and looked at her mother, the captain and then me, a wide-eyed look in her eyes. "You don't suppose, I mean," she lowered her lashes, and her lip quivered (she should be an actress), "that I could take Mommy's place?" The queen rose, trembling, and looked at all of us. "Oh my dear, you would do that for Mommy?" Big embrace, sob, sob. At no time did a tear escape either of their eyes. Then, looking to the captain, then me and then the dressmaker, the queen wailed, "Well, what do you all think? What? I know I can't make it–I'M SICK!" Just as you have probably guessed by now, the daughter took her mother's place and everything fit perfectly. Are you surprised? The audience loved it and marveled at how young and beautiful the queen was compared to all the other ladies in the court. Why, she didn't look a day over nineteen. And if you think the audience was surprised, you should have seen the look on Martha Washington and Mary Todd Lincoln's faces! I have told courts for years that when you use dirty words out on the floor, people can read lips, especially when they have opera glasses trained on you from the second balcony. Well I'm sure even the glasses got steamed up with what came out of Martha Washington's and Mary Todd Lincoln's mouths, the two sisters-in- law of the queen. They knew what had happened and were they FURIOUS! I thought those two would stroke out right then and there. However, the topping on the cake as it was, was about to happen while all eyes were on the beautiful young queen's entrance. The medical miracle of the 20th century had happened.

Unknown to everyone, except her own personal maid, the queen's mommy had made a miraculous recovery and was able to slip into a front row, box seat that had been reserved for a special guest of the queen. She had gotten strong enough to slip into a breathtaking, jeweled turquoise, beaded gown with matching shoes, long white, kid gloves and a rather casual mink stole. It all worked out beautifully, and everyone was happy except Martha Washington and Mary Todd Lincoln who, I understood later, put out a contract on both their sister-in-law and her daughter. I don't guess anything bad ever happened. I read the police reports every day.

Robert Goulet Autographed Your What?!!

This great story is told as Larry recorded it for me. I promise it's true, because I was in the limo with them and remember every minute even though I was only about eight at the time:

In 1965, a captain, of a popular ladies krewe, asked the actor and singer Robert Goulet, to appear as Grand Marshall in her parade. This was long before celebrities were regularly used as kings or grand marshals. It was my job, along with other special friends of the captain, to see that Goulet's lovely wife, Carol Lawrence, also a popular singer and actress who was very pregnant at the time, would get to the reviewing stands to view the parade. Mrs. Goulet was not prepared for the ride she got--six motorcycle escorts, two state trooper cars before and after the limousine, sirens blaring and roaring through the crowds and down one way streets the wrong way. To me, this was nothing, but Mrs. Goulet's stark white face and trembling hands clutching her belly told me she wasn't all that pleased. She was helped out of the limo and brought into the Mayor's office, where she had to lie down for a few minutes. I, meanwhile, went to the beginning of the parade route, where everyone was assembling and lining up, when all hell broke loose. Mr. Goulet had arrived to take his place in a convertible for the parade. He was such a hot item then as he had been in Camelot on Broadway with Richard Burton and Julie Andrews. His television appearances had women of every age, weight and size mad for him. The ladies in this krewe grabbed him, hugged him and waved papers and cards for him to sign his autograph. They nearly trampled the poor policeman guarding him. Finally, one little short, fat lady from the krewe, dressed like a clown, pushed her way in and got right in front of him. Gasping for breath, elbowing her competition, she yelled, "Mr. Goulet, Mr. Goulet, I love you. I play your song, "If Ever I Would Leave You," fifty times a day. I love you, but my old man hates you, and I tell him to shove it up his rear!" "Thank you, honey, thank you," he said. She continued, "I want your autograph, but I don't have any paper or anything, and these ladies won't give me nothing." Then she reached down and pushed up her rather large left breast. "Here, here, sign this! I'll never wash it, sign right here." And with a devilish grin, he said, "OK, darling, I will, but I have to kiss it first!" He did and then signed it to a mob of screaming women. Other screaming ladies decided they had all sorts of places for him to kiss and sign but the police and state troopers carried him off just in time. The captain was unaware of all of this as she had already taken her place in the parade which went on beautifully. Goulet loved the entire event. At the end of the parade he said he had never, ever experienced anything like it. Mrs. Goulet just smiled and was very gracious. I think she was probably just glad she didn't have her baby on her wild ride to the parade.

Larry, mother Irene Youngblood and Robert Goulet in 1965.

Beautiful Kings

More than once, one of Larry's kings, as you read before, was not only younger, but prettier than his queen. Pretty queens were hard enough to deal with, but a pretty king was a royal pain. For example, one man who was king of one of the larger ladies' krewes, was trouble right from the get-go. He didn't like the sketch, the color or the design, although it was never the king's or queen's decision, but it was the captain's word that was law. Here is how Larry told it:

King: I don't want a collar or anything tight around my neck.
Me: Well I guess I can change that.
King: Can I have it open to my waist so you can see my build?
Me: No.
King: Can I have short sleeves? I don't have any tattoos, and I have terrific biceps (he showed him).
Me: It's a tunic.
King: Well, I want a short one! I have great legs. You want me to take off my pants so you can see?
Me: Please, no!
King: I want everything to fit like my skin. Do you have a picture in your mind of what I want to look like now?
Me: Yes, your majesty, I have a perfect picture in my mind (I said this smiling).

Well, somehow it all came together. The poor dressmaker was the one who had to suffer through this agony more than me. The night of the ball, the ladies in the krewe, as well as the ones in the box seats, oohed and aahed and went all silly when the king appeared. He looked magnificent there was no doubt about it. As was the custom, the maids and dukes were already on the stage. The queen, a pleasant looking lady, was already on the throne. She sat looking gracious as the king proceeded to strut around the floor. There was no doubt about it; the king looked fantastic. Then it happened. The terrors of any Mardi Gras ball appeared. Three little boy pages between four and six, dressed just like the king, shot him down in flames. One couldn't find his momma and was crying, one who had was busy waving at her, and the third was doing kind of an Irish jig playing with himself because he forgot to go to the bathroom before the ball. The audience loved it. While all this was happening, the pages marched right up the back of the king's mantle, and he couldn't maneuver a turn because of the weight of the boys. His gleaming smile faded quickly, and he lurched back and forth nearly falling. The applause wasn't for him anymore, but for the small crying page who spotted his mother and ran off the floor into her arms where he announced at the top of his lungs, "I don't wanna be a 'pages' no more, I wanna go home!" The audience howled, and applauded wildly. By this time the king had tottered to the throne, a beaten man. The queen was suddenly radiant and smiled broadly as she acknowledged the audience. And why not? The little boy who didn't want to be a 'pages' was her grandson.

King, Krewe of Carrollton 1960's

King, Krewe of Carrollton 1950's

My God, the Queen's In Black!

As Larry became a more popular and sought-after designer, he also became more non-traditional and more daring with his queens' gowns, as you will read later.

The captain of a large men's parade krewe in the 50's was so pleased with Larry's work that he gave him full reign to create a theme, costumes, float designs and scenery. The captain already had his queen, a beautiful blonde with beautiful figure, a designer's dream. Larry chose, of course, what else but music of Broadway, Hollywood, opera and ballet. He combined them all. If the ball was about music, why not make the king and queen in black and white. A ball filled with the brightest colors of all, and then the king in white and his queen in black, with black and silver musical notes and rhinestones. This was a very new club from downtown New Orleans at that. They didn't care about what the upper crust would think.

He informed the captain of the theme, and he loved it. When Larry saw the queen, he knew he had made the right choice, so he proceeded. The court was portrayed as *The Follies, Knickerbocker Holiday, George White Scandals, The Boys from Syracuse, Louisiana Purchase, Lute Song, Madame Butterfly* and *The Student Prince*. The scene was ablaze with color, bright and brilliant hues. The captain was *Strike up the Band*, in red, white and blue.

The beautiful queen was in black velvet, cut in a trumpet line effect, with a black plumed collar, cut very low in front (Larry was always a cleavage man) and a black and silver mantle. The king was in white velvet, and once he was given shoulders, a trim waist and three inch heels in his boots, a black wig, beard and mustache, plus a strong tan, he looked like a movie star and a perfect contrast to the queen. But the audience simply didn't know how to react. They didn't know if they should clap their approval or laugh. The thing that caught the whole auditorium off guard was that the king came out first in white, and they assumed the queen would, too. She was a well guarded secret. Only the captain, the dressmaker, the queen, her mother and Larry knew she would be in black. When her costume was delivered to the auditorium, it didn't come with the others. As she made her way that night from her dressing room to the rear of the auditorium for her entrance, the late arrivals for the ball, as well as dozens of committee men who were in the hallways, stopped dead in their tracks. The talk went like this:

"Jesus, is the queen in black?"
"Oh, my God, the queen's costume is black!"
"Oh, they've gone too far."
"Unheard of."

"My dear, it's the most scandalous thing I've ever seen!"
"I don't believe it."
"Did that Youngblood person do this?"
"Get a program; he's through in Mardi Gras! Vulgar, awful, totally unheard of!"

The queen couldn't have cared less. She smiled broadly, stood tall and was very elegant. Of course, later Larry dressed queens in every color of the rainbow, as well as a rainbow.

Krewe of Bacchus

Most of the Bacchus chapter will be told in Larry's words:

Bacchus is a carnival club dear to my heart. Not only did I get to design it, I was also a charter member. The co-founder and member, Pip Brennan is a super guy and my closest friend. Why Pip, and his wonderful family, put up with me, I will never know.

It was decided when Bacchus was created, that it would be a club different from any other AND IT WAS! The floats would be spectacular and larger than floats were at the time. There would also be a celebrity king to reign, no queen, maids or dukes. That was somewhat of a disappointment to me as a designer, but I did get to design some great krewe, captain and king costumes. I really did want Pip and Dick Brennan, co-founders, to wear costumes that would be spectacular and different. I envisioned them in costumes of Roman influence and each driving a chariot with four white horses each. They would have looked magnificent and would have been a real hit with the crowd, no matter who was king. But they chose, instead, to dress like all the other officers on the title float, not a sequin more. And as you all know, the parade to this day is fabulous.

The celebrity kings really couldn't wear wigs and fake beards, because the crowd couldn't see them. So, creating the right costume for each king was a challenge. The king up there on that big float needed to be comfortable, but look terrific. Most were pleased with the results.

Bacchus to this day has no ball. It has a fantastic supper dance after the parade is finished. This took place in the Rivergate and later the Convention Center. There are as many beads and doubloons thrown after the parade as there are on the route. Little old ladies in evening gowns, furs and high heels scrambling for trinkets, it's a wonderful sight. There is live music, lots of partying and a lovely buffet. This goes on way into the wee hours of the morning. My famous last words after a Bacchus supper dance, "Oh, to sleep for a week."

Bacchus I – Danny Kaye

Who wouldn't want to design for Danny Kaye? Hans Christen Anderson, The Secret Life of Walter Middy, The Court Jester and, of course, White Christmas, were just a few of his delightful films. He was so talented and so popular, everyone loved him. What a thrill it was for me. Unfortunately, Mr. Kaye didn't feel the same. He really wanted Edith Head, the great Academy Award designer, who had done so many of his costumes, to design his for Bacchus. But when he arrived, he was told that they already had a designer with the design already completed.

I worked with the measurements he had gotten from the studio in Hollywood, and all I had to do was make a few adjustments because Mr. Kaye arrived just two days before the parade. Well, he was not pleased and it was not what he pictured. Edith always knew what he wanted. It was too short, he would freeze to death up there and he would have to wear long underwear under his tights because up there on that float it would be so cold. Edith would have done it this way or that. I was starting to dislike this great woman and had never even met her. I was broken-hearted but was getting angry, too.

Mr. Kaye said, "I might need an electric blanket up there on that float. Is there going to be a place to plug one in?" I replied with a big grin on my face, "Yes, I can think of several." And worse yet, he said he knew he wouldn't have any fun at all. Well, the rest is history. He sang, danced, waved his arms and threw kisses. New Orleans LOVED Danny Kaye and he loved New Orleans, who had never seen anything like Bacchus or their king. It was a triumph all around, for the krewe, for the city, for Mardi Gras.

The krewe costumes were well received and many thought them the most elaborate of any parade, bar none. But deep down inside, I was the only one still unhappy. Everyone was thrilled for me, but I still was a bit low because Danny Kaye didn't want my design. I carefully avoided him at the Rivergate, so much so, that I was one of the few members who didn't have my picture taken with Mr. Kaye, King Bacchus I. So, in the wee hours of the morning with the Rivergate still jumping, I gathered my mother and family and was getting ready to leave, when a policeman came up to me and asked me to follow him. My mother and I followed him to where Danny Kaye and so many others were gathered. Mr. Kaye said, "Oh, there you are my friend, and who is this?" "Your Highness, may I present my mother, Mrs. Peter Youngblood?" "You made a wonderful king, Mr. Kaye. I have always been a great fan of yours." "Thank you dear lady, and now everyone, may I present the designer of Bacchus and his mother. Larry is responsible for my beautiful costume as well as all the others." And with that, champagne was passed around. I was the happiest man alive!

About five years later, I met Edith Head who was in New Orleans for a charity style show. The host introduced me to her. "LARRY YOUNGBLOOD, OH MY! I saw pictures of Danny Kaye. Oh, they were beautiful. You are all he talked about when he got back to Hollywood." I, somewhat shocked, smiled (was in heaven) and said, "Oh, he really did?" She added, "And you are going to do a costume for Bob Hope this year. You'll love him! He's wonderful. Oh, I wish I could see it. It must be exciting to be a Mardi Gras designer, so different." This came from a lady who costumed all the leading stars in Hollywood and won several Oscars to boot. That compliment made my day. In fact, it made my whole year!

Bacchus II – Raymond Burr

To say that Raymond Burr, who portrayed Perry Mason, Ironside and countless other characters, was a bigger than life king, would be an understatement. He was big and jovial and had a wonderful sense of humor. Again, I worked from measurements sent to me, but as fate would have it, "Old Ironside" had gained a pound or twenty, and at a fitting he said, "What are we gonna do if it don't fit, Youngblood?" "Oh, don't worry, your Majesty, by the time the parade rolls you'll be fine." "Your Majesty," he laughed, "I like that. In my early roles before I got respectable as a lawyer, I was always the villain in those costumed epics, who was out to do his majesty in. I was mean. I hope no one wants to do me in." "Don't worry," I said as the dressmaker let out seam after seam to make his costume bigger. "They'll love you as much as our first Bacchus, Danny Kaye." Mr. Burr responded enthusiastically, "Oh boy, did he have fun. He told me there had never been anything like it in his whole life." And indeed, once the parade started, Raymond Burr found out what he meant.

Bacchus III – Jim Nabors

Jim Nabors, otherwise known as Gomer Pyle, was truly a delight to Larry. In real life, without the twang, he was a warm, witty gentleman with a natural, rich voice. He had a curiosity about his costume that prompted him to ask many questions. One of the joys of working with someone like Jim Nabors was the very earthy, natural way he got along with people.

Bacchus IV – Phil Harris

Phil Harris was a favorite of Larry's. Now that was a man who knew how to have a good time! Larry remembered seeing him first at the Blue Room in the Roosevelt Hotel when he was younger, and then listened to him on radio with Jack Benny on Sunday nights. An extra bonus was that he had gotten to be friends with his son-in-law who was in Bacchus from the start.

Phil was everything Larry hoped for in a king. It was fun from the moment they met. The fittings were a riot, and he kept everyone in stitches. They were on a first name basis from the start. None of that "Mr. Harris" or "Your Majesty" foolishness for him. He was as genuine as they come. Of course, he had his beautiful wife with him, Alice Faye. Larry had a crush on her since he saw her in *Alexander's Ragtime Band* (1938) when he was only ten years old. Larry saw all of her musicals four or five times, first for her and second, for the costumes, which were always so dazzling.

Larry began to get the hang of designing for night parades. The theme that year was *Bacchus Book of Horrors*, and he had a great time with the costumes for that one, mummies, werewolves, spiders and goblins. Al Hirt, Steve Stonebreaker of the New Orleans Saints and Larry were all witches. There had never been a trio of uglier witches in history, he later laughed. Harry James and his orchestra played for the gigantic affair at the Rivergate.

This was a special year for Larry, because my brother, Patrick Youngblood, had been chosen to be one of the pages on the king's float. He was ten years old at the time and was so excited. A night parade, high up on that big float, the excitement and a million people all screaming at once could be a bit scary for a little kid. But Mardi Gras was in his blood, too, and he handled it very well. My parents, Peter and Sera Youngblood, my Grandmother Irene and, of course, Uncle Larry thought he did a fine job. Needless to say, a good time was had by all. With Phil Harris as king, you couldn't go wrong.

King Bacchus IV, Phil Harris

Larry and King Bacchus XXII, Dennis Quaid, 1990

Bacchus V – Bob Hope

Larry thought designing for Bob Hope was like designing for an old friend of the family. Aside from being a very fine gentleman, comic and husband, his wife, Dolores, was a delight and enjoyed everything. Bob's costume had to be super special and, indeed, it was. And boy, did this man know costumes! He was aware of what went where, what the body can do inside a costume and hoped it would be comfortable. This man could put many a younger king to shame. He had bearing, good posture and knew how to wear a costume. Larry was terrified. He wanted Hope's costume to be super special and indeed it was. He used French silver and gold lame combined in a floral motif that was heavily encrusted in rhinestones and a heavy square collar of imported rhinestones. Stretch silver lame tights and silver boots were worn and the one-of-a-kind Bacchus crown of jeweled grapes and leaves. Larry was excited to hear that Bob later displayed his costume in his home for all to see.

One of the fondest memories Larry had was the private party given for Mr. Hope and his wife who were joined by Phil Harris and Alice Faye. The dialogue between Hope and Harris was priceless. They sang and danced, and Dolores and Alice sang. The men danced with each other's wives and then with each other. This would have made a great show in Vegas or on TV. Bob Hope the man, the entertainer and the King of Bacchus, sang his theme song, "Thanks for the Memories." Again, Larry had designed a costume for one of the greats. Edith Head said Larry would love Bob Hope and she was right.

Bacchus VI – Glen Campbell

Glen Campbell was one of the few kings of Bacchus with whom Larry spoke before he designed his costume. Campbell informed him he had skinny legs and did not want to wear any tights. Even on the phone, he was easy going and natural. Larry designed a costume, very western in feeling, an open collared shirt with puffed sleeves and an elongated vest, much like the men wore in the old west, and flare bottom brocade jeans over his boots, all worked in rhinestones. It was a laid back and comfortable costume, "Bacchus goes to the Grand Old Opry." Larry and Campbell both loved it. Apparently, Campbell was not a big drinking man, and no one told him that every time he toasted along the parade route, that he had to drink all the champagne in the Bacchus Cup and it's a pretty big cup! He couldn't stop singing. As Larry said, "He didn't roll into the Rivergate, he flew over it!" He was one happy king.

Bacchus VII – Jackie Gleason

Larry said of Mr. Gleason:

> *I was so excited about Jackie Gleason, otherwise known as 'The Greatest,' being the King of Bacchus. I would watch his show "The Honeymooners" over and over and never stopped laughing. Once again, we got his measurements from Hollywood and the dressmakers went ahead and got started. Well, the Jackie Gleason*

they made the costume for and the one met at the airport were two different people. He had been on a very strict diet and had lost at least 50 or 60 pounds. Gone were the big, jovial belly and the wonderful moon face. When I was introduced as his designer I told Mr. Gleason that since he lost so much weight one fitting was necessary to make adjustments to the costume. He told me very rudely that since I was the designer, I would just have to deal with it on my own and figure it out. He was just impossible and really didn't want to be bothered. I understood later that he hadn't been drinking or smoking, both which he was passionate about. That may have contributed to his attitude.

I chose a white and silver, wonderful Paliacci clown design for him with a gold jeweled ruff around the neck. The long tunic of imported brocade was in a diamond design completely encrusted with rhinestones and various colored lame set in the diamonds also worked with rhinestones. Of course, it was far too big for him and even last minute alterations didn't quite give the effect I wanted. However, everyone still thought it was so beautiful. The krewe members looked great and were in some of the prettiest costumes I had ever designed. I loved the circus theme. How could you miss with lions, tigers, aerialists, bareback riders and belly dancers to name a few? All in all it technically was "The Greatest Show on Earth" but the 'Greatest' wasn't that great.

Bacchus VIII – Perry Como

What can you say about Perry Como. He was simply the nicest man and so polite. He was warm and wonderful and with all of his success, a little shy. I didn't know if he ever felt comfortable in the elaborate silver brocade costume with a crisscross design of royal blue velvet across the chest and blue velvet sleeves. The whole effect was that of a Roman General, and quite formal, a lot different than his open shirt and sweaters he wore on TV. He was a prince about his fittings, was a small but trim man and so kind and considerate to all around him. He asked me, "Is this how you see me Larry?" "Mr. Como, that's how I see the King of Bacchus and that, is you." He replied, "Well, Bob and Phil told me I was gonna be fancy, but HOT DIGGITY, this is something else!" He smiled and looked in the mirror, "I hope they like it" (meaning the parade crowd). They were mad for their Bacchus Kings. Everyone loved

Perry Como. After seeing him all those years on TV he felt like a very special friend.

Bacchus Kings Through the 90's

Larry designed for the Krewe of Bacchus through the late 90's and loved every minute of it. There were many stories, not all funny and many that couldn't be repeated. Pip Brennan once told Larry that if he put down in print everything that happened during his designing career, Larry would have to leave town, assume a new identity and possibly be placed in the Witness Protection Program. Most of the kings with whom he worked were great and seemed to have a fantastic time before, during and after the parade and supper dance.

Pete Fountain as king was a classic. Who better than one of New Orleans own to be king? Harry Connick Jr., another great choice, really knew how to put on a show. Gerald McRaney was in awe of everything and was a genuinely all around great guy and gentleman. What can be said about Charlton Heston and Kirk Douglas? They were made for the role of King of Bacchus. Dennis Quaid was such a big kid, so excited to be part of Bacchus and Mardi Gras and really enjoyed throwing beads. Jean-Claude Van Damme was so happy to be Bacchus but REALLY LOVED his costume. He didn't get to wear that sort of thing in Hollywood for his roles. John Laroquette made the "Ninth Ward" and Larry proud when he was king.

Most of the Kings of Bacchus had one thing in common. They were in awe of the magnitude of Mardi Gras, having had no idea of the size of the crowds which were bigger than they ever imagined. Working on a closed Hollywood set or a stage was one thing, but being out there among millions of people yelling and screaming was something many of them were not prepared to experience. Of course, they loved it.

Being a member of Bacchus and designing for this club was the highlight of Larry's career in spite of the fact that Larry was not a huge fan of parades. He was all about the ball. On a more personal note, I have to say that he loved the people involved with the club since most were his dearest friends, and in many ways, his family. To Larry Youngblood, it was a great ride.

Larry and King Bacchus XXIV, Gerald McRaney, 1992

Bacchus Krewe Member, White Alligator

Bacchus Krewe Member, 1994

Bacchus Krewe Member, 1992

Bacchus Krewe Member, 1996

The Krewe of Elenians

The Elenian Club, a krewe of stunning young and married matrons, was already twenty years old when Larry was asked to design for it. The first lady captain had stepped down, and a new captain took over.

The costumes for this krewe were always a pleasure to design. The club didn't have a parade, so they concentrated on a beautiful ball. Larry's first ball with them in 1961, entitled *Bella, Bella Italia,* was appropriate since most of the members were Italian. They, like their male counterpart, The Krewe of Virgilians was the cream of the Italian society that was a part of New Orleans for many, many years.

The costumes were so colorful, representing the riches of Italy such as wine, music, scenery, sculpture and art. In the years that followed, they did themes such as *The Best of Broadway, Fete Des Bon Bons, Symphony of the Seasons, When Day is Done, Reflections of Yesteryear, Cinderella, Objects of Art and The Magic World of Roses.*

For their 1963 ball, *Fete Des Bon Bons*, Larry was a little worried. He had done a ball on a candy theme for the Krewe of Sparta, a men's organization in 1959, called *The Sweetest Ball of All*. Of course, he had to do something completely different this time. First of all, in Sparta, the theme had dukes in costume to represent the same thing as their maids. In Elenians, the dukes wore full dress suits, as was the tradition at the time of most ladies' krewes. For the maids, Larry was able to use different candy than he used in Sparta. A big plus was that each maid carried a long staff with the candy she represented. The candy was repeated in the headpiece, as well. The gowns were all full and featured the candy colors and designs in them as silver bells, bon bons, chocolate cherry delights, Easter eggs, Parisian mints, lemon drops, frosted marshmallows and English caramels. The whole effect was nearly all pastel and very lovely.

One of Larry's favorite Elenian balls was *Cinderella* done in 1967. By this time, he had already done two other Cinderella themes for other clubs, but this one was different. This was set in the late 15th century. It was a complete period piece, much more different than the other Elenian themes of the past.

Most captains stayed away from this time period, because the dresses were too heavy, too dark with huge sleeves, full skirts and strangely shaped headpieces. But Larry designed the costumes in bright colors of pretty pinks, yellows, lilacs and turquoise. All had wimples, turbans and crowns with contrasting chiffon or organdy veils that were lighter and flowed freely when the maids moved. They wore elaborately jeweled panels down the front of their costumes and sleeves heavily worked in sequins and stones. The captain was the Fairy Godmother and the ball was a huge hit.

Maid, Krewe of Elenians, 1960's

Captain, Krewe of Elenians 1960's

Queen, Krewe of Elenians 1960's

Krewe Member, Candy Corn, Krewe of Elenians 1960's

Maid, Parisian Mints, Krewe of Elenians 1960's

Maid, Lemon Drops, Krewe of Elenians 1960's

The Krewe of Hypathians

Here are Larry's highlights of the Krewe of Hypathians:

I designed the Krewe of Hypathians in 1950 as a last minute replacement for their designer who, at the last minute, went to New York. This was a smaller krewe of about two hundred women. It was a very pretty ball, a salute to Stephen Foster and was not a real challenge. There were pretty ante-bellum gowns, big hats and lots of ruffles. The captain was an older, very dynamic woman who was a no-nonsense, a little rough around the edges type, but very nice. She had been in Mardi Gras a long time. She was a former maid and queen of the bigger clubs when she was younger. I found her warm and witty.

She wanted her theme for the following year to be Famous Queens in History; Queen Elizabeth, Mary Queen of Scots, Katherine the Great, etc. However, for the queen she wanted something really fantastic and totally different, something that had never been done before. This statement was to haunt me for years to come. This queen was to portray The Queen of Sheba. The lady who was to portray Sheba was about 38 or 40. She was the kind of woman who was pretty when she was young, but as she grew older became even more voluptuous and alluring. She was a brunette with brown eyes that were almost black. The captain said she wanted something dynamite on this lady and to go wild – a very bad thing to tell a healthy twenty three year old bachelor with a warm respect for women.

The costume I designed for her was what I called "a drop dead look." When other women saw it they wished the queen would drop dead. And when men saw it, they thought they might. Remember, this is 1950, and most Mardi Gras queens were very traditional in white satin or silk, trimmed in gold or silver, jeweled collar, A-line, semi-full, full or empire gown, but not for Sheba. After all, the captain told me to go wild and that's just what I did! First of all, the dress was in two pieces, unheard of for queens of Mardi Gras balls, ever.

The top was a jeweled bra of silver lame worked in rhinestones and rubies, tiny straps of stones went over her shoulders and dropped at the top of her arms with dangling red beads. Her skirt of silver lame fit like the skin on a sausage and was slit several inches above the knee and was lined in red silk and intricately worked in red stones and rhinestones. Instead of a traditional crown, she wore jeweled serpents woven into her hair with pearls and rubies falling from their mouths, and to finish it off, a ruby in her navel. When the captain saw the sketch, she couldn't catch her breath and had to sit down. When she composed herself, she said three words, "GO FOR IT!!" Later, when she saw the finished costume on the queen, she asked, "Can we get away with this, do you think?" The queen looked at herself in the mirror, smiled and answered the question herself, "Honey, if I can't wear this, I won't be queen!" That settled, I told the captain that the entrance would be a problem because the Queen of Sheba would never have just walked out onto the stage. She would have been carried out on a litter by slaves, four, big, black men in little leopard skin sarongs and jeweled turbans with lots of baby oil on their bodies so they would shine.

Now the captain thought I had really gone too far as she downed a shot of bourbon the dressmaker brought her. She said, "Jesus, Youngblood, they'll run us all out of town on a rail! I don't know if even I could pull this off. I'm a pretty wild, old broad, and I don't give a damn for all this traditional crap, but a half naked white woman being carried out by four half naked negroes, Christ you're gonna have us all sent to Angola!" She started laughing then said, "Well, why not. Hell, Mardi Gras was on the dull side before the war and not much better after. I saw those escapades with Camilla LeDuke in balls you designed. They put a little spark in Mardi Gras. That's when I noticed you, honey. Who else would have had the guts to dress a maid as an oyster on the half shell and make her look good yet?" That settled, I got four young, black, extremely well built, male college students from one of the local black colleges. And so the night of the ball came, and everything was going smoothly.

The queen always dressed alone. No one knew who she was or had seen her gown. In another part of the auditorium were four black litter carriers. They were polite, well mannered young men who thought this was a neat way to earn $25 each for an hour of work. Well, the lights dimmed to exotic music, and as it started to build up, the announcer roared, "The Queen of Hypathians portraying the Queen of Sheba, all hail the Queen!"

First there were about six well endowed young ladies in their harem costumes. They came out with urns, jeweled chests and swinging incense –beautiful, all about 16 to 18, then about six more sprinkling rose petals in front of the queen. They had very little on and were very seductive as they rolled around the floor. Then with the crash of a huge gong and a wild drumbeat, the queen made her entrance, carried on her litter. There was a gasp of shock through the audience. Some ladies just stood there with their hands to their faces, some just sat right down. And then it started; the applause, very polite at first, then louder and then a roar to the top of the auditorium. Everyone was talking. Some of the older, old guard committee men showed their disapproval by simply folding their arms, some even more so, by turning their backs and leaving, gathering their poor dazed wives out of their box seats. I could hear things like, "Spectacular," "Never saw anything like it," "Exquisite," "Vulgar," "What bad taste," "Unheard of," "She has ruined our ball," and "He has ruined his career!" No one had ever seen a ball like this and a ladies club at that. I was standing upstairs next to the current New Orleans District Attorney at the time, who told me he was concerned because of the black men, half naked black men at that. I simply told him that this was art and we were recreating a scene from ancient history. After all, Sheba was in the Bible, I told him very respectfully.

The District Attorney knew he would catch hell about it. Two uniformed policeman made their way through the balcony of gapping committee men to talk to the D.A. who said he would be down shortly. His last words to me that night that I will always remember were, "I want to talk to you later, Youngblood."

New Orleans at that time was still segregated. Once the litter carriers deposited Sheba to her throne, they bowed on their knees and carried the litter off and that was that. The auditorium was in such a roar, you could hardly hear the music as the announcer called out the names of the dukes. Finally the king, a handsome, very well known state politician appeared. The audience began to settle down. The mood changed. A wild drumbeat began and a fabulous couple appeared. They were young dancers about 20 years old. Both had been sprayed silver and wore clusters of grapes here and there, very small grapes. The dance was very sensual and passionate. The audience loved it. The ball was a huge success, and suddenly, I was grabbed, back-patted, hugged and told that it was sensational, that it could have been a Hollywood production! But some diehards said that kind of thing could ruin Mardi Gras and the Krewe of Hypathians. The captain, who was thrilled, simply told them to, and I quote, "Kiss my rhinestone ass!" I did hear after that several prominent people were all for having the captain, queen, the four black men and yours truly arrested for indecent exposure, nudity in public and a few other offenses. We weren't, of course.

Captain, Krewe of Hypathians, 1950's

The Krewe of Hypathians - The Muses

Larry recalled:

It was hard to top Sheba. Later, the same captain wanted another classical but different theme. She chose The Muses. I'm afraid I was like most people who lived in New Orleans. I didn't realize when I was young that a whole set of streets uptown were named for the Muses, and each one was a goddess from Greek Mythology and stood for something special. The only thing I ever thought of was how damn hard they were to pronounce much less spell. Of course for me, who always loved a challenge, I wanted to do something really different. But this time I think we will leave the shocking part out of it. Some people still had not forgiven me for Sheba. So I started doing the research on the Muses.

Their everyday existence was simple; life was sex, fun, games, sex, games, sex and, of course, time out for eating and drinking. I needed a diagram to figure out who was fooling around with whom, but I finally got the gist of things. The Muses were the daughters of Zeus and Mnemosyne and each Muse was bestowed with a neat little gift of her own. They are Calliope, Goddess of Poetry and Eloquence, Euterpe, Goddess of Music, Erato, Goddess of Sacred Poetry, Clio, Goddess of History, Melpomene, Goddess of Tragedy, Thalia, Goddess of Comedy, Terpsichore, Goddess of Dance, Uranie, Goddess of Astronomy and last, but not least, Polyhymnia, Goddess of Oratory. I'm still not sure about her. She doesn't get a fair shake like her sisters. I was having a tough time coming up with ideas but knew each headpiece would tell the goddess's own story with every maid dressed in a different color.

One day I was up in my studio working on the watercolor sketches of the maids. Each maid had her theme and motif wound around her classic hairdo of the time--and then it happened. In one sketch, the color ran off the design and into her hair. I watched the pink of the design wash over and quickly took the paint brush and made the hair the same color as the gown and headpiece. Pink hair--this could work, I thought! I made the headpiece a deeper pink and the accent designs in gold. I was so excited. This all happened by accident. The concept of hair matching gowns and headpieces was different, but would the captain go for it? Why couldn't the Muses have green, lilac, blue and pink hair? I wanted another opinion.

I ran down two flights of stairs, yelling all the way. "Mother, Mother, wait till you see this!" As usual, she was in the kitchen cooking. She was quite used to my atomic outbursts when I had a new idea. Out of breath, I said, "I've got it, I've got it." She looked up completely unruffled and said, "Good son, whatever it is, they want four boxes of it at the Port of Embarkation." Puzzled, I said, "What? The Port of Embarkation is twenty blocks away." As she laughed, she said, "I know, they heard you all the way down there. Calm down 'blue eyes' and show me what you're working on." She gave me her opinion, which was always good. She loved the idea but hoped the maids would wear more clothing than Sheba. The captain loved the entire concept. The ball was a huge success, other captains were impressed, and as a result, I picked up many new customers, partially due to my runny watercolors.

Maid, Christmas, Krewe of Hypathians, 1950's

The Krewe of Virgilians

The Krewe of Virgilians was a large club consisting primarily of Italian men. The balls were beautiful and the costumes spectacular. Opera and Biblical themes were often created for this fantastic club. Money was never a concern because there was plenty of it, plain and simple. Larry designed for Virgilians in the past, but never attempted anything of the scope of *The Ten Commandments*, in 1960. There were more costumes than he had ever designed for any single ball theme. When you watched a Virgilians ball, it was more like a Hollywood production than a ball. As Larry explains it:

> *If a club was going to spend a small fortune for its production, I wanted everything to be as authentic as possible. In the scene of "The Ten Commandments," where the baby Moses was found in a basket by Pharaoh's daughter, the princess, the captain wanted to use a doll for the baby. I wanted a real baby. The captain, though concerned, agreed. He told me that the audience would still think it is a doll. How would they know it is a real baby? I replied, "Pinch it lightly, it will cry." The princess did, the baby cried and the audience bought it. A doll would never have cut it for me.*
>
> *One of my all time memories was a scene where Salome performs "The Dance of the Seven Veils" for Herod. Salome was not a maid in the ball, but a Special (not a krewe member), a dancer from one of the big, dancing schools that performs in the ball tableau. Well, this young lady was a stunning young Italian girl of sixteen or so. She was perfect for the role of the seductive Salome. She had dark brown hair, was tall and lovely.*
>
> *I worked with the choreographer and had a tape of the music the dancer would use. I decided she would work the veils from cool to warm colors, to red hot, to an illusion of nude. The ball got underway, and the announcer boomed out that Salome, to please her wicked mother Herodias, was told to dance for Herod, and he would grant her any wish, and she was to ask for the head of John the Baptist on a platter. The orchestra began the wild drumbeats and very sensuous music. Salome appeared. She took center floor and was completely covered in a purple, jeweled chiffon sari effect, the only thing you could see were her eyes, her hands and her bare feet. Off came the purple now exposing the royal blue chiffon scarf from her shoulders. Herod was an older man, wide eyed and enjoying every minute of it. To a wild drumbeat, she turned and turned so you could see all the other brilliant colors. She dropped*

the blue then a green scarf to the floor. She had on a jeweled bra with all the other colored scarves hanging from her waist. She went into a wild belly dance, which caused Herod to sweat profusely. A few of the men in the audience were, too! The lime scarf flew into the air, then the red, and all that remained was the orange chiffon over the flesh.

Now, as Salome stood at the bottom of Herod's throne, who was by this time clutching both arms of it, the sweat pouring from his face, she did a few little turns and dropped the orange scarf. The audience saw flesh as she lay on the steps in front of Herod. They gasped for breath, convinced that they were seeing their first nude in the history of Mardi Gras, but she was wearing a jeweled bikini plus her bra. Then two of Salome's hand maidens rushed out and covered her with a beautiful white chiffon robe, heavily jeweled. The poor Herod stood up on very shaky legs and clapped three times. Two young men, portraying white slaves, came out with a tray covered with cloth. No one had seen it before, not Herod or poor little Salome, not even in rehearsal. She took the cloth off and was supposed to smile.

Well the way it happened was, John the Baptist's head was a mannequin head with a wig. I made the eyes bulging out of their sockets, his tongue hanging out of his mouth, all very realistic and covered with shiny fake blood. Well, old Herod let out a yell and fell back onto his throne, and poor Salome, when she saw the head, let out a blood curdling scream and fled the stage. The audience, the ladies in the box seats and call-out section screamed, too. The big red stage curtains were closed and the house lights were turned up until the audience and others could compose themselves. The line to the ladies room was fantastic, and the ball wasn't even over yet. Once everything was under control, the ball proceeded. It turned out to be a spectacular success.

Larry received much acclaim on this one particular ball and for other Virgilians productions for many years. He was pleased that so many people still remembered and appreciated his work. To Larry, the designs he created for the Virgilians were the finest of his fifty-two year career.

Egyptian Guard, Krewe of Virgilians 1960

Dancer, Salome, Krewe of Virgilians 1960

Herodias, Krewe of Virgilians 1960

Maid, Japan, Krewe of Virgilians 1961

Queen, Krewe of Virgilians 1960's

King, Krewe of Virgilians 1960's

Maid, The Great Deluge, Krewe of Virgilians

Larry at the exhibition of his costume designs in 1999.

Retrospective

Larry was passionate about his chosen career and loved what he did for over 50 years. He was definitely born at the right time. The Mardi Gras industry was changing, and he was right there to contribute. While this book highlights only a part of his colorful life, it provides insight into what was, until now, an unknown part of Mardi Gras history. In spite of the fact that he could no longer draw after his stroke, Larry was creating costume design in his head right up to his death in 2007. His art and influence will define Mardi Gras for generations to come and hopefully inspire those embarking on the same or similar artistic career path. A huge talent in his field, he is greatly missed.

Mardi Gras balls and parades Larry designed for throughout his career from 1946-1998

Adonis	Alhambra	Alpheus	Ancient Scribes
Anubis	Arabi	Argus	Aurora
Bacchus	Bal Masque	Caputainians	Carrollton
Christopher	Cynthius	Diana	Druids
Elenians	Elks	Eurydice	Freret
Golden Age	Helena	Hera	Hypathians
Iris	Jupiter	Les Marionettes	Maids of Troy
Naiads	Nemious	Okeanos	Orion
Orpheus	Pandora	Patria	Pegasus
Sonians	Sparta	Virgilians	
Washington D. C. Ball	Zeus		

Costume Design for the Theatre

Kiss Me Kate	The Boy Friend	Good News
High Spirits	I Can Get It for You Wholesale	Tovarich
Mame	My Fair Lady	Gypsy
Lil Abner	Annie Get Your Gun	Bus Stop
Fantastics	Bells Are Ringing	Bye Bye Birdie
Do I Hear A Waltz	South Pacific	Applause
Of Thee I Sing	LA. Purchase	The Sound of Music
West Side Story	Gentlemen Prefer Blondes	Guys and Dolls
The Pajama Game	All the King's Men	Arsenic and Old Lace

Costume Design for Opera

Cavalleria Rusticana (3 times)	I. Pagliacca	Suor Angelica
Madame Butterfly (twice)	La Boheme (3 times)	Tosca (3 times)
Lucia di Lammermoor	The Barber of Seville	The Marriage of Figaro
La Traviata (3 times)	Gianni Schicchi (twice)	Falstaff
Faust		

Costume Design for the Ballet

Ballet from Sampson and Delilah   The Nutcracker

Note: All photographs, articles and costume sketches used are from the private collection of Elizabeth Y. Canik

www.ingramcontent.com/pod-product-compliance
Lightning Source LLC
Chambersburg PA
CBHW051416070526
44584CB00023B/3450